How Architects Visualize

How Architects Visualize

Tom Porter

 VAN NOSTRAND REINHOLD COMPANY
New York Cincinnati Toronto London Melbourne

To Holly

First published in the United Kingdom by Studio Vista, a division of Cassell Ltd.
Copyright © 1979 by Tom Porter
Library of Congress Catalog Card Number 79-9713

ISBN 0-442-26149-7 (cloth)
ISBN 0-442-26150-0 (paper)

Printed in Great Britain

Published in 1979 by Van Nostrand Reinhold Company
A division of Litton Educational Publishing, Inc.
135 West 50th Street, New York, NY 10020, U.S.A.
Van Nostrand Reinhold Limited
1410 Birchmount Road, Scarborough, Ontario M1P 2E7, Canada

16 15 14 13 12 11 10 9 8 7 6 5 4 3 2 1

Library of Congress Cataloging in Publication Data
Porter, Tom.
  HOW ARCHITECTS VISUALIZE
  Bibliography: p. 115
  1. Architectural design.   2. Architectural
design—Data processing.   3. Communication in architec-
tural design.   I. Title.
NA2750.P65   1979   729   79-9713
ISBN 0-442-26149-7
ISBN 0-442-26150-0 pbk.

Contents

Acknowledgements

I would like to thank the following for their invaluable help in preparing this book: Keith Albarn, Fred Batterton, Faber Birren, David Bonsteel, Geoffrey Broadbent, Ian Davis, Charles M. Eastman, Martin Gordon, Ron Hess, Nigel Hiscock, Kenneth Illingworth, Mike Jenks, Stuart Lewis, Claude Lubroth, Andy MacMillan, Ted Odling, Richard Padovan, Iradj Parvaneh, Victor Pasmore, Nick Phillips, David Reed, William Taylor, William Tilson, Victor Vasarely, Charles D. Wheelwright, Ken Whiting.

Special thanks are due to Conway Lloyd Morgan.

Graphics: Sue Goodman. Additional material by Mike Conn and Janice Broad.

I would also like to express my gratitude to the following First Year Architecture students at Oxford Polytechnic who contributed project work: Paul Cook, Paul Johnston, Stephen Palmer, Peter Risbey, Gordon Shaw, Graham Stirk, Ian Taylor, Teresa Thomas, Stephen Willacy.

Introduction

'You learn to see by looking. Drawing insists that you look.'
Jim Dine

Many books have been written which claim to teach the architectural student how to draw or, at least, how to record his mental concepts on the drawing-board. The majority of such books preach, not a drawing method which relates to any visual experience, but a 'drawing-board style', i.e., an artificial language of spatial coding. They appear highly seductive to the unwitting student because, in presenting an easily imitated and superficial formula, they short-circuit any profound experience.

Architecture, however, is concerned with the physical articulation of space; the amount and shape of the void contained and generated by buildings being as material a part of its existence as the substance of its fabric. Other disciplines such as painting and sculpture are equally involved with spatial organization but in different terms. In that the role of the architect has gradually become more and more specialized, he has still to cope with the spatial variables of light, surface, shape and form although in almost complete isolation from the influence of other artists. As a consequence, he has adopted a private and mainly graphic language of design which is more concerned with technique than with any experiential understanding of space.

This pictorial stylism can describe a world perceived through standardized eyes; a strange, drawing-board world in which a colourless architecture is hatched against line and dot backcloths whose monochromatic bleakness is occasionally punctuated by stereotyped cars and trees or, more rarely, by odd, balloon-shaped beings who attempt to bring life and scale to the starkness of their settings. In adopting such a stylized form of expression, a student risks delegating his visualization of space and the objects which occupy it to common stereotype; one which is becoming as universal in its conformity and professional use as is the blandness and anonymity of the architecture it procreates. We have only to consider the visual inadequacies of the modern environment or the findings of research programmes which examine its psychological effects to discover mounting evidence that uninformed methods of representation can not only influence the formation of ideas but can predetermine the appearance of resulting architecture.

It is against such a background that this book has been written, and in the awareness that design attitudes in education are often founded on the assumption that architecture is born within the confines of a sheet of paper. Beyond an historical survey of the changing modes of spatial representation, its central aim is an understanding of the nature of space. Throughout the text a series of related projects are introduced together with a variety of physical and non-physical spatial concepts, a study of the elements governing spatial perception, a critical assessment of the perceptual viability of conventional design codes and, finally, a review of the alternative methods of externalizing spatial ideas together with a glimpse of the future. None of the projects is 'Architectural', i.e. concerned with the design of buildings; however, they are all architectural in that they aim towards an essential grasp of space through an experience of its many constructs and structures.

Realizing that a first-hand, conscious experience of space is important in the training of those who intend to articulate it, Leonardo da Vinci devised a series of games for his junior draughtsmen. For example, in order to develop visual accuracy in judging dimensions, he proposed that a line be drawn on a wall and, standing approximately seven yards away, his students attempt to judge its length by cutting a straw —the one who cut his straw nearest the actual length won the game. A further diversion recommended by Leonardo involved judging depth by guessing the number of times the length of a thrown javelin was contained in the distance of the throw. Although Leonardo's games were intended to sharpen the visual skills of budding artists, it is even more critical for the environmental designer who employs a graphic design dialogue to engage in a direct experience of space.

Before embarking on any of the following projects, the participant should not be inhibited by any lack of drawing ability because the act of drawing is entirely based on the creative act of perceiving —a 'good' drawing being purely the extension of an understanding of the nature of that experience. Anyone can draw, even without previous practice, providing they can hold a drawing instrument and allow it to respond, not to superficial techniques for their own sake, but to a critically perceived event. For instance, the author's late father had no facility or need of drawing but could, when encouraged, produce the most sensitive pictorial representations of horses. This singular ability stemmed from his close working relationship with horses for, as a farmer and blacksmith, he commanded a profound knowledge of their complex anatomical forms: knowledge he was able to co-ordinate in the act of drawing.

The importance of achieving a concentrated co-ordination of the links between mind and body was recognized by Johannes Itten —the Swiss artist who exerted such a revolutionary influence on design education during the 1920s. His method of 'tuning' his students was to begin the studio day with early-morning physical exercises on the Bauhaus roof, followed by a short prayer-meeting. Although meditation and physical jerks lie beyond the parameters of this book, its projects are deeply concerned with exercising links between eyes, brain and hand; exercises which, in helping explore the experience of space, function as a form of mental gymnastics in which aspects of our perception are pre-selected and studied.

The ensuing projects are grouped in three sections; each section being intended as a jumping-off point into related design fields such as history, visual perception and behavioural psychology, experimental simulation and philosophies of basic design. Any reader wishing to go further into these areas can do so by referring to the notes and the bibliography. The materials required for participation in the projects are a sketchpad —minimum size A4 $11\frac{1}{4}$ by $8\frac{1}{4}$ inches —pencils, pens, brushes and a basic colour range of paint. Any other media needed are noted at the beginning of each project.

1   Short History of Spatial Representation

'Space: that which is not looked at through a keyhole, not through an open door. Space does not exist for the eye only: it is not a picture: one wants to live in it.'

El Lissitzky

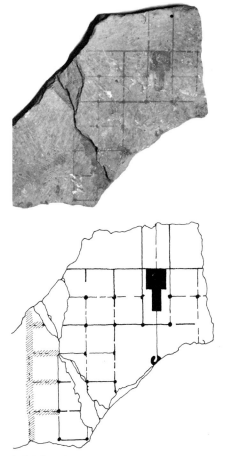

1 (a) Landscape architect's ink sketch plan for a grove fronting the XIth dynasty temple at El-Dier el-Bahari. Sandstone 42 × 30.5 cm. Courtesy The Metropolitan Museum of Modern Art, Museums Excavations, 1920–22, Rogers Fund, 1922.
(b) Drawing after the original published in the *Bulletin of the Metropolitan Museum of Modern Art*, New York, 1921–22.

The immediate conversion of architectural ideas into two-dimensional 'models' has not always, it seems, been central to the creation of the built environment. In more traditional structures—such as the Shinto temples in Japan and Nelson's flagship H.M.S. *Victory*—construction was eyeballed, worked directly into space entirely without the aid of any working or design drawings. The ancient Chinese builders of Ming and Manchu cities also worked without scale drawings, relying instead on intricate small-scale plaster models which display a remarkable precision and elaboration.

The depth of spatial understanding in primitive and ancient cultures still perplexes modern science. For example, the meaning behind the Peruvian 'Lines' and the internal workings of complex labyrinths of space within some pyramids still remain unsolved despite the repeated probes of modern archaeology. The mystery surrounding the origins of such an ancient and profound command of space has triggered a plethora of speculation which ranges from the sensational idea of an extra-terrestrial instruction to the theory that prehistoric man was endowed with a sixth sense. The latter refers to the notion that our early predecessors could tune in to electrical force-fields which enabled them to undertake extended journeys into the wild for food and flint. Set against this is the theory of lay lines first proposed by A. Watkins in 1925. He suggested that a landscape systematically littered with notched hillsides and strategically positioned stones shows that men moved with a full-scale 'map' of the environment. A remarkable grasp of an auditory plan of space is reflected in Professor Richard Carpenter's account of the Alaskan Aklavik tribe who can graphically record an accurate impression of the shape of islands at night by listening to the sound of waves lapping their shores.

The evolution of this link between graphics and concepts of space in environmental design overtures can be traced back via a continuous, though threadbare, chain of evidence to the higher cultures of the Near and Far East and the Mesopotamian and early Egyptian dynasties when the idea of an architectural ground plan had already been developed and spatial concepts were organized against simple linear grids. The earliest preserved drawings illustrate that such a system was already in use in Ancient Egypt where roughly scaled plans—elevations being much rarer—were drawn in black on small papyrus sheets squared in red. Also, preparatory linear devices for the compositional arrangement of size and shape have been detected beneath Egyptian tomb painting. They were later to be dissected by the surgery of Constructivist and Neoplastic artists, such as

1

Piet Mondrian and Theo Van Doesburg who saw them as architectonic ends in themselves, and whose clear structures of geometric order were to have such a pruning effect on twentieth century architectural thinking.

Amongst the earliest known 'architectural' design drawings is a landscape layout plan for a tamarisk grove which fronted the Egyptian temple at El-Dier el-Bahari near Memphis. It is drawn in ink on a sandstone flake and dated *circa* 2100 B.C. This particular drawing is remarkable as it shows how little the linear drafting of space has changed during the last four thousand years. More interesting is Geoffrey Broadbent's speculation that the designer, possibly for the first time in the history of environmental design, made a crucial drafting error (fig. 1). His enthusiasm for the grid plan carried him away for he had extended the network into a neighbouring site; subsequent archaeological excavation, however, discovered that his mistake was confined to the drawing as the actual grove was contained within the boundary of its original site.

However, in attempting to penetrate the mysteries of the ancients' methods of visualization, some other studies find it unlikely that preparatory drawings were widely utilized in architectural design. If only half of the modern theorists are correct, the Great Pyramid, Stonehenge and other ancient monuments were built exclusively according to scientific needs. Their location, setting, size and shape were determined by the need to embody cosmic measures and ratios and they functioned as huge astronomical clocks predicting eclipses and verifying disputed measurements. These theories are founded on the idea that designers only require a method of representation if the appearance of the outcome is of importance. The more we uncover about the design approaches of the ancients, the more we find that they were concerned less with appearance than with responses to esoteric and cabalistic figures. Concern for the visual appearance of buildings in anything other than applied decoration seems only to have arisen when aesthetics became a subject separate from metaphysics and philosophical speculation, and addressed itself to the visual, the subjective and the fashionable. It is almost certain, therefore, that the Egyptians, Greeks, and Romans built in relation to their sacred canons before pleasing their own aesthetic sensibilities.

This is supported by an investigation by the archaeologist, J. J. Coulton, who suggests that it is unlikely that ancient Greek designers produced scale drawings of the plans and elevations of their temples because, within a technology lacking fine calibration, drawings in scale for such massive structures would have led to inaccuracies in their construction. A striving for precision in the widespread repetition of architectural components and buildings appears to have been more central to their visualization of space than any relationship to the immediate environment. This contrasts with the sentiments of Vitruvius who wrote: 'The look of a building when seen close at hand is one thing, on a height it is another, not the same in an enclosed place, still different in the open.' However, in suggesting that designs should be adjusted accordingly, Vitruvius was referring to Roman buildings which were often designed through a use of scale models. Greek temples, on the other hand, being erected in isolation and on artificially levelled platforms, were never controlled by the nature of their settings (fig. 2).

If it is accepted that the Greek architect designed against proven proportional systems (for these existed long before their philosophical theories had been elaborated by the Pythagoreans) it is likely that rules were formulated in such a way

2

2 Unfinished Doric temple sited on its plateau at Segesta, Sicily. Photo: William Taylor.

that they were 'portable', being applied as buildings went up, with little detailed design beforehand. If preliminary drawings were used at all, Coulton thinks, it was more likely that they were for smaller parts of buildings, for there is considerable evidence of a widespread use of 'paradeigmata', full-scale specimens of the more elaborate elements such as capitals. From these mock-ups builders could extract detailed dimensions with callipers, thereby achieving repetition from replicas without any need for scaling up or conversions.

However, intriguing accounts of a developing sophistication in graphic representation in the Hellenistic period are to be found in the writings of ancient commentators such as Democritus and Vitruvius. As part of the evolution of the accurately drawn plan and elevation, they describe an innovation called Skenography —a method of creating illusions of depth in fourth century Greek theatre stage sets. This method was also described in a book written by Anaxagoras based on the practical experiments of the scenic artist Agatharchus. According to the commentators, Skenography was later developed into a form of perspective drawing called Aktinography the mechanics of which were subsequently mysteriously lost to civilization. Its existence is also mentioned by Plutarch who, in connecting Agartharchus' achievement with its adoption by architects such as Phidias, describes the consequent increase in the speed with which buildings — such as the Parthenon—were raised. Vitruvius explains that Aktinography was a spherical rather than linear perspective—his justification being the entasis in the columns of the Parthenon. This implies a use of preliminary perspective drawings, for the design of such curves (to remove the optical effect of dead-weight and

3

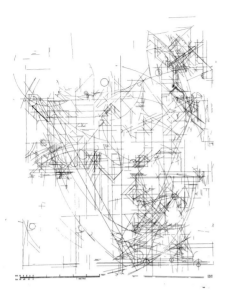

3 Drawing by John H. Harvey of the tracing floor at Wells Cathedral. Originally published in *The Archaeological Journal*, Vol. 131, 1974. Copyright: John H. Harvey.

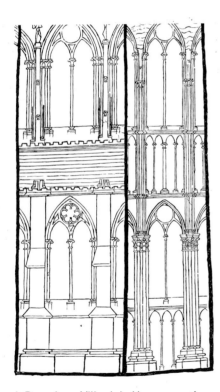

4 Page from Villard de Honnecourt's sketchbook showing his attempt to depict two elevational planes of Laon Towers, France.

reduce the visual imbalance of an overhanging entablature) involves a mastery of freehand drawing. In any event, the Greeks' understanding of perception evidenced by their subtle modification of buildings is unequalled, even by a modern environment which is riddled with optical illusions. It is of interest, however, that the design of the Parthenon might have been influenced, at least in part, by an artist's discovery.

Plans, as such, were not used in the design of Western European architecture until the rediscovery of Euclidean geometry in A.D. 1100. Without this geometry the forms of Gothic cathedrals would not have been possible because for the first time medieval architects, being committed to the Pythagorean concept of 'all is number', were able to set out accurately a plan against a network of repeated units and, again by modular geometry, project sections and elevations.

From the remnants of evidence available it appears that the basic representational methods used in the planning and elevating of architectural concepts became firmly established in the Middle Ages. However, there are significant differences in the degree of dependence placed upon various techniques and in their use within the building process, some of these distinctions exerting a variety of spatial effects in the creation of buildings. For example, the medieval architect was a designer who, like his ancient counterpart, enjoyed a profound command of space because he worked directly in space. He would base his three-dimensional concepts of potential buildings on architectural forms contained within the library of the existing built environment, using other buildings as full-size models or specimens which could be studied and then modified or refined. As an artist in his own right and with a practical knowledge of materials and construction, he was able to utilize design aids such as modular geometry and drawing instruments much the same as those in use today. When he employed a drawing it was often executed to large or even full-size on tracing-boards or on a specially prepared plaster screed floor. It was only for small-scale details that he drew on vellum on a trestle board —the precursor of the modern drawing-board.

Discounting the common claim that designers in the Middle Ages used little or no design drawings, J. Harvey in his account of medieval building offers several arguments to explain their limited survival. He suggests that beyond their immediate utility there was little reason for the architect to retain them; that the large tracing-boards and plaster screed tablets were rubbed out (although an elevation drawn in plaster survives at Wells Cathedral (fig. 3)), and that parchment was such a valuable commodity that it was recycled for other uses such as bookbinding. Perhaps his strongest argument is that design techniques were considered to be secret and such secrets were well concealed within the Guild societies. In order to illustrate this secrecy, Harvey recounts the unfortunate killing of Bishop Conrad in 1099, assassinated by a zealous master mason who had learned that the Bishop had uncovered a secret method for waterproofing the foundations of St Mary' Church in Utrecht, the Bishop's own church! However, some plan and elevation drawings do exist. Among the earliest known are those preserved in the 1335 sketchbook of the French architect Villard de Honnecourt (fig. 4).

The influx of Greek ideas into medieval draughtsmanship simply sharpened the experiential skills of the vernacular builders who had, hitherto, developed an architecture in which a representational method was not necessarily a prerequisite of construction. In this traditional context the 'designer' was the builder, a craftsman directly in control of building operations. Spatial concepts were carried completely within his 'mind's eye'; his architectural vocabulary evolving along a trial and error basis but being directly linked to natural conditions and measured against anthropometric needs. Superimposed against this profound comprehension of space the architect-craftsman emerges from the ranks of builder-craftsmen, pausing during construction to translate his concepts into crude plans and incomplete, fragmented elevations. But drawings of entire buildings were not made, perhaps just for lack of technical skill. Yet, the spontaneity with which the great Gothic churches spring up against gravity and the sky suggests they were never fully put down on paper. They arose unforeseen.

The Gothic architect worked thus within a comparatively safe and familiar architectural style until 1284 when the roof fell in on his attempts to defy gravity with the collapse of Beauvais Cathedral. Until then the total appearance of buildings had not been of prime importance for, even as late as 1301, the vaults of Milan Cathedral—felt to be too steep by a cautionary Commission—were modified through a mathematical approximation of Pythagorean triangles. A divine proportion was what was sought, and into that equation neither visual appearance nor the weight of stone finally entered.

Until well into the Middle Ages, architectural space was evolved in this way; the medieval architect would take long journeys —even travelling abroad—in order to study and measure the essential proportions of 'full-sized specimens' of buildings which had initially been admired and selected by his patron for adaptation. The later introduction of a wooden scale model served only to communicate his intentions to the client and also extract a detailed estimate of its cost. By the end of the Gothic period models of parts of buildings were made, possibly for testing purposes. One form of model-making used as a design tool was the paper cut-out, which could demonstrate patterns of vaulting ribs and be bent by the medieval designer in order to simulate the intended structure of a space.

By contrast, his Renaissance counterpart had no such sure frame of reference as he was bent on an architecture inspired by a rubble of Graeco-Roman components, the apparent success of which was to provide a design-kit par excellence for the next five centuries. The only way he could test out the feasibility of these more dynamic visions was to build working models, sometimes in the actual materials he intended to use. It was, therefore, common practice to develop architectural concepts in the round by constructing large prefabrications in wood, clay or stone. These were not used purely for structural experiment as in the Middle Ages, but as design aids in the visual orchestration of mass and space. For example, Filippo Brunelleschi primarily invented in three dimensions and sometimes built his preparatory constructions to one twelfth of their proposed scale. In Leon Battista Alberti's *Ten Books on Architecture* is a description of the type of model he found useful in his design process. He writes: 'I would not have the model too exactly finished, not too delicate and neat, but plain and simple —more to be admired for the contrivance of the inventor than the hand of the workman.' Michelangelo also prefabricated full-sized wooden models of parts of his buildings as a visual check and, in a letter to Vasari complaining of an error which had developed during the erection of one project, he explained that it had arisen, '. . . even though I had made an exact model, as I always do'. Vasari also documented Michelangelo's design sequence for the cupola of St Peter's in Rome which began with a clay model

5 Replica of Michelangelo's large-scale preparatory wooden model of his design for the cupola of St. Peter's, Rome. Courtesy Musei Vaticani.

along with plan and section sketches; this initial phase led to the construction of a large wooden model (which took one year to complete) through which its final form was achieved (fig. 5).

The most significant event during the Renaissance was a development in the pictorial representation of space. Earlier attempts to organize the recession of planes into graphic illusions of depth through crude isometrics and axonometrics (sometimes in combination with plan views) can be found in ceramic and wall painting from the Greek period onwards. But the invention (or rediscovery from Arab mathematicians such as Al'hazen) of perspective marked a crucial turning point. Designers suddenly realized that they could translate their visual perceptions into an apparently comprehensible and manipulative series of delineated spatial events, capable of accurately rendering a design intention. Together with the evolution of the plan and elevation, linear perspective was a further projection of the geometry which was at the essence of the ancient design philosophy.

Although Al'hazen's treatise on perspective —which recognized that we see an object because each point of it directs a ray into the eye —was annotated in Latin by Lorenzo Ghiberti, it was Brunelleschi who first pioneered its practicability in two perspective panels (now lost) in 1417. Antonio di Tuccio Manetti is attributed with the earliest documentation of the invention which he tells us was made in a drawing of a view across the Piazza del Duomo, Florence. Manetti describes this means of depiction as a process of peeping from the back of one of his panels through a hole bored at its centre at a mirror held at arms length. In this fashion, his viewpoint was controlled so as to coincide with the vanishing point of the reflected picture image. Manetti also described a second attempt made in the Piazza of the Palazzo dei Signori in which Brunelleschi covered the area above his drawn buildings with burnished silver. When this perspective was viewed in the mirror through the peephole, the drawn image combined with that of a reflected, natural sky.

However, a seminar held at Plymouth Polytechnic in 1978 set out to re-appraise the Renaissance literature which documents the invention. This raised several questions both as to the venue and the method of its innovation. Firstly, that although biographers such as Manetti and Vasari agree that Brunelleschi's initial experiment recorded a view of the Baptistry of San Giovanni seen from the doorway of the Cathedral of San Maria del Fiore, it was unlikely that he would have selected this subject-matter, this assumption being based on an event which occurred just a few years previously when Brunelleschi lost the competition to design the bronze Baptistry doors to his arch-rival Ghiberti. A second question also concerns the position from which he is reported to have made the perspective drawing. If Manetti's estimation is accurate, recent calculations show that Brunelleschi could not have clearly perceived the view he is believed to have drawn. But, in fairness to this biographer, it is not always easy to pinpoint precisely the exact position from which a building is painted.

Suspicions are also aroused in the disparity between the accounts of Manetti and Vasari together with the fact that Alberti —although accrediting Brunelleschi with the discovery in *Della Pittura* —did not describe its geometry. By contrast to Manetti's account of the use of mirrors and peepholes, Vasari writes that his perspective was achieved in an 'unaided' manner being geometrically constructed by tracing the intersecting lines between ground plan and elevation. J. A. Lynes

6

suggested that Brunelleschi himself might have perpetrated the confusion when, in supporting his claim to have invented perspective, he exhibited his two panels possibly without any explanation of their geometry. This medieval-like secrecy would have been in keeping with his character for he is reported to have advised: 'do not share your inventions with many'.

One interest Brunelleschi did share with his contemporaries was a fascination for sundials which, incidentally, function using co-ordinates inherent in perspective drawing. It is the analogy between viewpoint/picture plane relationships in perspective and gnomon/scale relationships in sundials which gives rise to some interesting speculation. If Brunelleschi had used mirrors, a far more elegant solution to his problem would have been to fit a horizontal gnomon into a hole at the centre of a silvered panel. This procedure would avoid the intrusion of his own reflection and allow him to stand back and align his sight with the point of the gnomon and the mirror image of the selected view. In later removing the gnomon he could then peep through its socket from the back to a further mirrored image of his drawing and experience an unreversed, single-point perspective.

J. A. Lynes concluded that it was not beyond the realms of impossibility for from the static, central viewpoint which, together with a pure linear dissection of the picture plane, became absorbed into Renaissance architecture's search for an transferring perspective co-ordinates from a view through glass to a wooden panel. However, enthusiasm for this invention concretized into an identifiable school of 'perspectivi' and early paintings which employed it such as Masaccio's frescoes for the Brancacci Chapel in Florence had holes drilled at their centre which, it is assumed, held a peg from which strings could be attached for marking the vanishing lines (fig. 6).

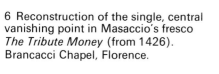

6 Reconstruction of the single, central vanishing point in Masaccio's fresco *The Tribute Money* (from 1426). Brancacci Chapel, Florence.

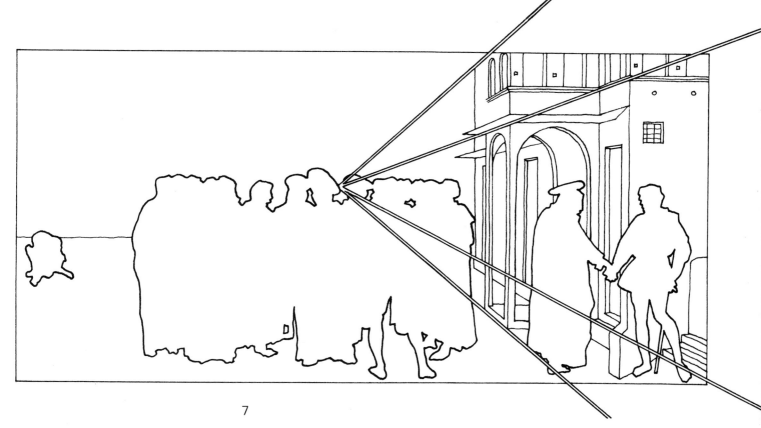

7

7 Cityscape. Courtesy Vredeman de
Vries: On Perspective, 1599.

Cellini, in relating perspective to sculpture, finds shortcomings in its power to depict a three-dimensional figurative object; Vasari accuses the painter Uccello of wasting too much of his creative time in his obsession for its refinement in his work. The Renaissance architects had little use for careful, detailed representations for, by today's standards, as Fred Scott observes, they accepted a considerable sketchiness in the design process. He writes: 'There is a sense that the grandest buildings could be realized with fewer drawings than we would need today in the conversion of a small terraced house.'[1] Nevertheless, this innovation was to trigger a shift of emphasis towards a two-dimensional depiction of architectural concepts and it led to a fashion for drawing visionary images of buildings and even whole utopian cities (fig. 7). However, the penetration of space through Brunelleschi's delineation positioned the architect outside his concept by placing distance between the viewer and the viewed —the very word 'per-spective' means through-seeing which refers to the drawing as a window or, in the ancient Greek version, of looking into a stage-set. This conceptual stance of looking into or at a two-dimensional illusion of space had not been the case in pictorial treatments of all cultures. For instance, in oriental art vanishing lines radiated away from the spectator into a wider concept of space —a reversed perspective which, in positioning his mind's eye behind the picture plane, allowed the artist to visualize from 'inside' his concept. As a system of representation, Brunelleschi's perspective was a contradiction to the very nature of visual perception as it caused

8

its user to freeze in time and space. Its inherent symmetry and straightness resulted from the static, central viewpoint which, together with a pure linear dissection of the picture plane, became absorbed into Renaissance architecture's search for an ideal geometrical unity.

Glass, first discovered by the Egyptians, was another technology that was to further the movement towards humanism during the Early Renaissance as it was to affect concepts of spatial visualization. Lewis Mumford, indeed, has described the transition between the philosophies of the medieval and Renaissance periods in terms of the gradual purification and subsequent clarification of window glass. Medieval symbolism, represented by the brightly coloured stained-glass of cathedral windows began to dissolve into the clear glass of the fourteenth century allowing an unimpeded view through to the form and colours of nature, a naturalistic perception characteristic of the beginning of new thought in Europe. A new and sharply focused world was also framed by the glass of spectacles which, in adding additional years to eyesight, had boosted the revival of learning. By the sixteenth century the invention of the microscope and the simultaneous improvement of telescopic optics had, on the one hand, rocketed the vanishing point into outer space and towards infinity; on the other, it had, in the words of Mumford: '. . . increased almost infinitely the plane of the foreground from which those lines had their point of origin'.[2] In this way, Mumford explains that glass had shattered man's naive conceptions of space and extended his perception of an expanding world. However, a world viewed through the glass of windows, spectacles and optical instruments is a framed perception —the very impression reinforced by the parallel development of linear perspective.

Up until the Renaissance, buildings had been conceived as total works of art created by 'artist-craftsmen' who had orchestrated the urban environment as a fusion of habitable space (architecture), the elaboration of form (sculpture) and of planes of colour (painting). With the advent of humanism and resultant thirst for knowledge during the Quattrocento came a creative outburst which led to the gradual separation of architecture and art into distinct avenues of study. Each branch of intellectual activity became isolated one from another and a building, a piece of sculpture, and a portable painting existed in their own terms. The 'fine artist' became committed to an art for art's sake while the architect drifted towards an intellectual process of design which was to become firmly rooted in developing skills and conventions for drafting space. It was the conventionalization of figuration techniques which preoccupied draughtsmen for they became more concerned with how a building should be drawn than what was visualized; in this way, architecture became increasingly affected by methods of depiction. Within this bifurcation into specialisms, linear perspective was to become petrified in the deep-freeze of architectural design processes while it became a model for experiment throughout the subsequent development of painting. Almost as soon as its laws were formulated, artists such as Leonardo da Vinci began to disrupt its unnatural rigidity by introducing several vanishing points and horizons into one picture and also discussed its perceptual modification through a use of stereoplastic colour.

As the architect began to shed his creative dialogue with three-dimensions and work almost entirely with graphic means, the model assumed a different role from that given it by Brunelleschi, Alberti and Michelangelo. By the seventeenth century

9

it had become an explanatory device rather than an exploratory tool. For example, when describing its use, Sir Christopher Wren considered the model less for his own benefit than that of builders or client. He wrote that '. . . a good and careful large model . . .' should be constructed for '. . . the encouragement and satisfaction of the benefactors who comprehend not designs and drafts on paper'. As an adjunct to a visualization process in which drawing had become a language of the initiated, the new role of model-making represented a further step away from any wholistic conceptualization of space. This shift of emphasis was reflected in the high degree of finish of models and was synchronous with a movement towards the communication of external appearance for its own sake.

The most significant shift to a purely graphic expression of space at both the levels of design and communication coincided with the emergence of the architectural profession in the eighteenth century. This event heralded a growing concern for fine-line drafting skills in which technical drawing was considered to be tantamount to an art form. Aesthetically, the architect had become less concerned with the sculptural qualities of form and space and had, instead, turned to designing in terms of the pictorial nature of façade and silhouette and, in communicating these concepts to others, even the 'presentation model' was to be superseded for a time by the infamous 'artist's impression'. Also, the growth of the print medium had encouraged a proliferation of ideas through publications which had meant that, by 1900, drawing had finally become the acceptable language of the architect.

This obsession with drafting techniques and beautiful drawings was to survive a series of broadsides over the years from such active theorists as John Ruskin, William Morris, and later Henry Van de Velde and Walter Gropius. The attacks came at a time when design schools such as the Ecole de Beaux Arts were extolling virtuoso draughtsmanship as the key to architectural elegance. In rebelling against the remoteness of paper designs from the real world of work, Gropius founded the Bauhaus in 1919 and devised its revolutionary curriculum in the hope of resurrecting the medieval 'lost chord' between designer and craftsman. Although its programme included the study of plane geometry and drafting techniques one tutor, Laszlo Moholy-Nagy—a Constructivist with a predilection for the dynamics of light—encouraged his students to employ as a design tool a simple, partly transparent model which he called a 'space modulator'. He explained that this was intended to provide his students with an opportunity of relating concepts to materials '. . . as against previous architectural methods in which structural inventions were hampered by the shortcomings of visualization on paper alone'.[3]

Linear perspective was to be completely abandoned in the early twentieth century by the Cubist painters who, influenced by Cezanne's perceptual rationale of form, Kepler's cine camera and primitive African abstractions of space, experimented with the portrayal of the whole structure of any given object and its position in space (fig. 8). Cubism, contemporaneous with Einstein's theories, introduced the concept of time into art and Picasso's experiments with the dynamic interpretation of transparent planes brought a new sensibility of space in terms of our trajectory through it. Picasso's preoccupation with the totality of perception influenced architects such as Gropius and Le Corbusier to adopt for completeness the axonometric drawing—a characteristically cubic diagram which induces its

8 Georges Braque, *Oval Still Life (Le Violon)*, 1914. Oil on canvas, 36¾ × 25¾ in. Collection, The Museum of Modern Art, New York. Gift of the Advisory Committee.

user to assume a hovering, almost godlike view of his conception. As opposed to linear perspective which encouraged looking through and up at the interiors and exteriors of architectural space, axonometrics pushed the viewer's stance upwards, causing the visual erosion of the corners of buildings (fig. 9). It is interesting to note that the researches of the artists Agartharchus, Brunelleschi and Picasso into models of spatial representation had, at respective points in time, influenced the

9 Bauhaus workshop wing. The adoption of axonometrics forced the design stance upwards. The resultant need for the 'mind's eye' to penetrate its cubic interior possibly caused the erosion of corners of buildings.

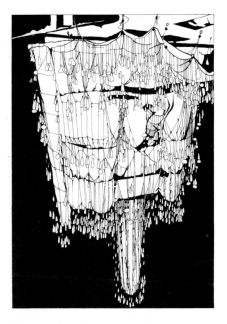

10 Drawing of the inverted canvas and wire model through which Anton Gaudi studied the structure of his design for a future church.

11 The fluid, dynamic foyer space of Eero Saarinen's T.W.A. Terminal Building, New York. Photo: Ezra Stoller.

12 *Opposite*
Architecture as an art form. *The Little House in the Clouds*. Four drawings by Stanley Tigerman, assisted by Tim Sullivan, of a project design which is half architecture—half topiary.

articulation of built environment—the last affecting a post-1920 architecture in which both exterior and interior are simultaneously visible in a transparency of floating, glassy planes.

In this context of relating representational methods to the appearance of architecture, it is worth mentioning the design approach of Antoni Gaudi; a designer of unquestionable genius and whose visualization methods were as unconventional as his architectural forms. His designs for the Church at Santa Coloma and Sagrada Familia in Barcelona did not include graphic techniques but were evolved through a series of inverted wire and canvas models, worked out with the engineer, Eduardo Goetz and the sculptor, Bertran (fig. 10). He rarely drew plans and relied almost exclusively upon three-dimensional forms of visualization—a method which rather than inhibiting creativity, had increased his capacity for articulating highly complex space. Gaudi's grasp of space was reinforced by workshop experience and a feel for materials which echoed that of the medieval architects.

It is this essential grasp which marks off the important twentieth century architects as creative designers who visualize and articulate spatial concepts in an imaginative and unconventional manner. A random study of their formative experience and design methods discloses a conceptual process which, being founded upon an understanding of the potential of space in all its manifestations, transcends a simple reliance upon an anonymous drawing-board stylism. For example, in the book *Eero Saarinen on His Own Work*, the author describes his own visualization process which replicates that of Michelangelo—first modelling of space in clay before any graphic interpretation. Saarinen explains that the plasticity of the form of his T.W.A. terminal in New York could not have been achieved on paper alone (fig. 11). A break with the rigidity of graphics we associate with traditional drafting is embodied in the highly personal and expressive graphics of Eric Mendelsohn and Oscar Neimeyer. Or Le Corbusier who

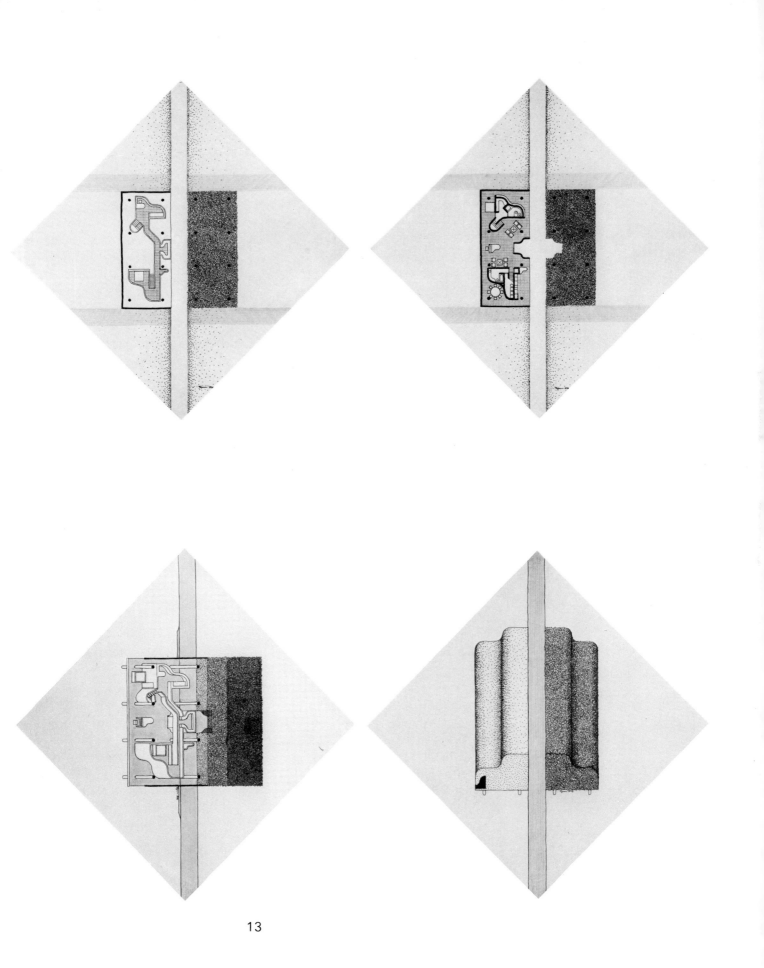

13

like his Renaissance counterpart was an artist in his own right, although he had only the use of one eye: as part of his Venice Hospital Project, he drew to full-size an exploratory section through a ward space on his studio blackboard as a means of judging its implications as realistically as possible. Meanwhile, in adopting a more sculptural approach, Luigi Nervi's concrete organic froms have remained fluid beyond the drawing-board by being subjected to a medieval-like modification during the course of their construction.

However, in tracing the shifting roles of three and two-dimensional modes of visualization along broader spectrums we find that, after 1920, the Modern Movement's rejection of a Beaux Arts academism had paralleled a revival in the use of scale models. These were enlisted for the three-dimensional 'sketching' of a purist and uncluttered space. These white cardboard models miniaturized, presented and proliferated the new International Style—causing the model-maker's craft to be mirrored in a built architecture stripped of ornamentation. By the 1960's, the advancing coldness of a pseudo-scientific approach was to spawn a fashion for a new kind of model—the mathematical model and the interaction chart which furthered the systematic reduction of any profound spatial experience.

In its hankering for an earlier heritage of spatial richness and diversity, a post-Modernist movement has restored the influence of the architectural drawing beyond the level of a window on the design process and, indeed, elevated it to a work of art. The current obsession with graphics in environmental design has seen the formation of schools akin to the grouping of ideologies amongst Renaissance artists. Such groups include the New York Five and the O.M.A. (Office for Metropolitan Architecture) whose work is exhibited as objet d'art in the international art market. These works comprise elaborate perspectives, colourful axonometrics and emblematic plans (fig. 12). In welcoming the return of a graphical architecture, Robert Stern suggests that its revival was triggered by an exhibition of drawings selected by Arthur Drexler from the archives of the Ecole des Beaux Arts and mounted in New York's Museum of Modern Art in 1975; others suggest that this superficial craze merely reflects a fanciful unbuilt architecture forced by the recession of Western economies.

From this survey of the design of space and the changing interaction of two and three dimensions in its articulation it should be clear that, since the Renaissance, the architect has gradually developed away from direct spatial manipulation and, instead, increasingly invested in graphic interpretations of his ideas. This emphasis on drawing, either as an enrichment or reduction of architectural concepts or as a convenient vehicle for spatial codes, has been at the centre of architectural education throughout past decades. This places a tremendous responsibility on the young designer to understand the implications both of the limitations and creative potential that drawing can have on his spatial thinking. Usually the student imitates graphic conventions such as the 'non-spatial' languages originally devised to communicate purely dimensional information to the builder without exploring alternative avenues of expression.

With the inherent dangers of this situation, the need to understand the spatial potential of drawing —in its many forms —is paramount: as a means of creating feedback from spatial experience, as a vehicle for quickly exploring ideas, and, in context with other modes of representation, as a dialogue between three and two dimensions.

Notes
[1] Scott, F. 'Pictorial and Sensual Space' *Architectural Association Quarterly* Volume 8, No. 4, 1976.
[2] Mumford, L. 'Agents of Mechanization and the Eotechnic Phase' *Environment: Notes and Selections on Objects, Spaces, and Behaviour* Brooks/Cole, California, 1974.
[3] Moholy-Nagy, L. *Vision in Motion* Theobald, Chicago, 1961.

2 Sensations of Space

'A perception cannot be drawn. The form must be imagined immediately before this. The conception can, if sufficiently clear, guide the creative process known as drawing.'

Sven Hesselgren

1. Architecture as Space

Within design education philosophies concepts of space and form are usually separated and regarded respectively as the negative and positive of the physical world, a world where solid objects reside and void—the mere absence of substance—is a surrounding atmospheric emptiness. However, since the beginning of the nineteenth century, there has been an alternative concept of space as continuum, as the continuously modified surface skin between the pressures of form and space in which the shape of the space in our lungs is directly connected to the shape of the space within which we exist (which is, in turn, just a layer of the space surrounding our planet). Architecture, therefore, can be considered as a creative expression of the co-existence of space and form on a human scale but its understanding, together with all other concepts, is rooted in the psychological space of our thoughts. Meanwhile, as a consequence of experimental psychology studies, space has become more dynamic and tangible. As a result of attempts to understand the mechanics of perception, research findings begin to inform the designer as to the nature of its many forms. The need to develop an awareness through graphics of the 'form of space' as an element vital in itself becomes the central issue of this chapter which, in examining various concepts of space through a series of projects, is intended to encourage what is lacking in contemporary environmental design—the essential grasp of space.

Our perceived experience of interior and exterior architectural space is primarily a sensual event involving movement—for to pass through an environment is to cause a kaleidoscope of changing sensations, of transitions between one spatial impression and another. Each experience affects the orchestrated functioning of our senses in a variety of ways—our eyes, ears, nose and skin registering changing stimuli which trigger a flood of brain responses on all levels. For example, a visit to a funfair can provide a gamut of heightened response through unusual and extreme sensations of space. Helter-Skelter, Carousel and Big Dipper offer exhilarating opportunities to spiral, spin and undulate through space at speed; literally breathtaking experiences. The fairground environment is also filled with exaggerated levels of sound, smell, taste, and touch together with amplified volumes of form and colour for 'all the fun of the fair'. By comparison, to enter a medieval cathedral is to experience a contrasting perception in which the sights, sounds and smells of the hubbub outside are replaced by a new range of sensations monitored by our body. The skin registers a reduction in temperature,

15

the eyes accommodate both to lower levels of light and to intense coloured light from stained-glass windows, the nose detects musty and sometimes mysterious odours and the ears pick up the echoes of isolated sounds against the concentrated stillness of a vast, cavernous space.

The richness of spatial diversity is all around us in the natural and man-made environment and, indeed, in relationships between the two. We can experience unlimited space from vantage points on high ground and tall buildings, partially defined space from within canyons and streets, and totally enclosed space from inside the scooped-out depths of caves and subways or from within the confines of windowless rooms such as elevators. Each experience is modified by the prevailing conditions under which it is perceived, be it midday light or dusk, rain, snow or fog. As a facet of this experience, architectural space is subject to a whole series of perceptual overlays: day-night and seasonal cycles which cause it to be alternately illuminated by light from the sun, its reflected light from the moon and artificial light sources. Also, depending upon its climatic setting, it is subject to extended periods of warmth, cold or changing air pressures. We could experience architectural space as a kaleidoscope of kinetics teeming with darting shadows, racing clouds, fluttering flags, the rise and fall of colour saturation, vibrations of growth and decay and, the essential ingredient, milling human beings living out their lives. The dynamism of this concept is generated by our movement about a vast global time-machine which is actually travelling at approximately one thousand miles per hour —the speed at which the surface of our planet spins in space as it follows its orbit around the sun.

2. Perceptual Space

'Tactile space separates the viewer from an object and visual space separates an object from an object.' Georges Braque.

As we move through space each body, neck and eye movement sets the visual environment in motion. We can look up, down, and sideways and collect information even at the periphery of our field of vision; we can adjust by focusing on points in the far distance and points near at hand. Of all the sense organs the eyes receive spatial information which is, both in frequency and velocity, far in excess of any other. The physiology of the brain indicates that the visual scanning process is capable of monitoring up to eighteen separate images every second. Nevertheless, despite the importance of vision we should never ignore the involvement of the other distance receptors: hearing in relation to the acoustic properties of space, and smell in aiding identification and orientation; the immediate receptors (skin, membranes and muscles) being more subtle in their sensitivity to temperature, humidity, texture and shape. The combination of these varied sensory inputs reinforces, elaborates and may even alter our visual perception of the environment to give us a complete image which, in turn, can be modified by our own personality and motivation.

Much of our understanding of environment is experienced through the sense of touch yet, except when the more radical aspects of physical comfort and discomfort are involved, there is probably little conscious awareness on your part of the sensation of handling this book, the chair on which you now sit, or the support on which your elbows rest. As designers, our articulation of space could be far richer if we became only slightly more aware of the tactile sense —which leads us to the first project:

Project: Points of Contact (a tactile space sequence within a room)
Using a comic-strip format in your sketchpad, compile a tactile space diary based upon a consciously experienced chain of touch sensations within one room. This is simply to catalogue in words and diagrams the variety of surfaces and textures encountered by pre-selected extremities of your body during a short period of time. For example, your diary could monitor a sequence of skin contacts from any of the everyday rituals we perform such as washing and grooming in the bathroom, dressing in the bedroom, or eating breakfast in the kitchen (the reason for focusing on early morning activities is because there is less likelihood of garments impeding our sense of touch).

   The primary aim of this project is to experience tactile sensations in a considered and introspective way, recording each sensation within the sequence as:

(a) a thumbnail sketch of the source, or a detailed blow-up drawing of its surface —or, whenever possible, a frottage (pencil rubbing) taken directly from the surface.
(b) a record in words of aspects of individual sensations associated with each texture, i.e., its temperature (the cold shock of initial contact with a lavatory seat or the warmth of washing water), its surface quality (the silky smoothness of soap or the comparative roughness of a towel), and its substance (the give of a toothpaste tube or the inert hardness of a plastic toothbrush handle) together with your subjective interpretation of its experience in terms of pleasantness and unpleasantness.

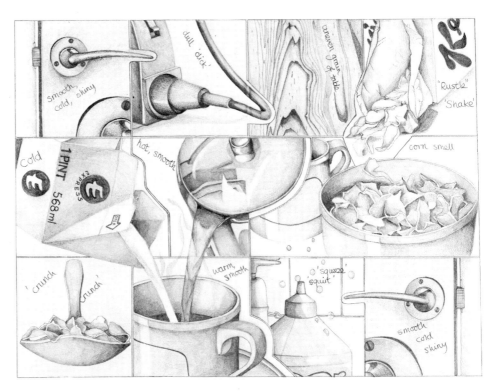

1 Student project exploring tactile sensations encountered during breakfast.

17

(c) an observed relationship between each tactile experience and information collected by the other senses, e.g. smells, tastes and sounds in relation to each substance or surface (fig. 1).

It would be wise to plot first a simple sequence of finger-tip or feet sensations whilst dressing or moving about the floorscape of your bedroom, for the increasing complexity of this kind of investigation becomes apparent when we begin to monitor the introduction and operational levels of the other senses in respect of further activities. In the bathroom, for instance, we bring into effect the senses of touch, sight and smell when using soap, deodorants and scents —adding taste to our experience of toothpaste. Whilst eating we experience a fascinating interplay of touch-sight-smell-taste which accompanies a wide range of textural information detected by our fingers, lips, tongue and the lining of the mouth. It is, therefore, suggested that the tactile sense remains central to your investigation and that, whenever possible, other sensory impressions are related to your heightened awareness to the sense of touch.

One method of fine-tuning a concentration on tactile experience is to close the eyes —a dampening down of the visual sense often unconsciously used as a means of gaining heightened response to the other senses such as when listening to music or love-making. Similarly, a hungry person will screen off other senses to enable him to find food using a much more acute sense of smell. The Colgate toothpaste 'ring of confidence' is a further example of screening or masking an olfactory space which, in a society embarrassed by bad breath, allows closer contact between people —Arabs, however, accept body odours and can identify them with emotions. A key aspect of this project is to discover that tactile and visual experiences are closely interwoven and, as experiments into sensory deprivation have shown, even though we can temporarily disconnect ourselves from sight, sounds, odours and tastes, we can never be free from tactile sensation for we have always the pressure of our body on the surface which supports it.

In designing a house for a partially sighted client, the American architect Charles Moore undertook a project which had met with reluctance from other designers daunted by the thought that its user would never see the result. Moore's response to this problem produced a design which articulated textures, smells and breezes to act as locational messages. Air conditioning and heating systems were not installed because of the occupant's dependance upon his sense of touch and smell —allowing him to orientate through sensations of sun and shade and from scents of grass, orchards and two indoor gardens, signalled by the direction of air moving through the house. Orientation around interior space is also aided by the sound of trickling water from an indoor fountain and heavily contrasting areas of colour and textures on walls and floors. More subtly, Moore included a series of rooms of changing size and dimension which, ingeniously functioning as sounding chambers, reverberate ambient sounds from which his client can locate. The rooms are connected by a paved hall and corridor system which twists and turns like an ancient street. This incorporates a snaking wooden guide rail which is shaped in section exactly to match a handrail his client previously discovered in an airport —the tactile quality of which felt right to him.

Moore's design for this house (fig. 2) accentuates the kinesthetic aspect of our tactile appreciation of space, i.e., space primarily perceived through the skin and

2 Opposite
Interior of New York house in which the volume of non-visual signals were amplified by architects' Charles Moore and Richard B. Oliver for their partially sighted client. Photo: Norman McGrath.

3 Controlled irregularity in an Oriental garden space. Photo: M. Keswick.

muscles and in response to our position within or movement through it. Oriental designers are also particularly aware of the subtle relationships between visual and kinesthetic space for, in a culture where living space is at a premium, they can stretch experience through a masterly manipulation of irregularly positioned textures and objects which necessitate an increased and correspondingly irregular number of muscular sensations (fig. 3).

Our bodily contact with the edges of space is central to our awareness of ourselves and spatial location. It seems important, therefore, that as designers of environment we should base future man-made space upon some understanding of its contribution to the experience of others rather than subscribe to the common attitude found in art galleries where, in being politely discouraged from touching sculptural objects, we might be forgiven for believing that form and its surface elaboration is something to be sensed purely through the eyes!

3. Perceptual-Psychological Space

The next project concerns itself with an observation of the behaviour of occupants of differing types of interior space and an introspection of ourselves in relation to each space. As in the previous study, a comic-strip or grid format will suffice as a vehicle for documenting the aspects of this investigation in your sketchbook.

20

Project: The Shape, Sound and Dynamics of Space
Select three different kinds of interior space:

(1) a small, confined space (such as a waiting room, elevator or a railway compartment).
(2) a large and lofty space (such as a cathedral, an auditorium or a gymnasium).
(3) a public or private space which is related more to the sphere than the cube.

After selecting your three interior spaces, plan to spend up to one hour in each with your sketchpad. Within each space make three sets of observations:

(1) The Shape of Interior Space —draw a thumbnail plan and section, adding a scale figure inside the latter in order to establish relative size. The perceptual stance of making these diagrams is interesting because, in being part of each space, the act of horizontally and vertically delineating its contours stems from your physical presence within the interior thus placing your mind's eye inside each drawing. In other words, the plan and section lines will surround your spatial concept—an experience to be developed in future drawings.
(2) The Sound of Interior Space —make written notes and/or sketches which describe both the range of materials which define each interior together with a description of characteristic sounds which the size, shape and surface tend to reverberate. Different shaped rooms and different materials produce differing acoustic effects. A bathroom, for example, being filled with resonant materials such as porcelain, water and glass creates an excellent sounding chamber for an early morning whistle or song. In other parts of a house this acoustic quality is dampened by sound-absorbing surfaces such as carpets, curtains and wallpaper and, of course, people. Similarly, the acoustic properties of different kinds of public interior space varies —we have only to compare the sound of a cough in a cathedral, an elevator, and a circus tent.
(3) The Dynamics of Interior Space —draw a second, larger plan and within it make diagrammatic notes of how people appear to arrange themselves both in relation to each other and to the periphery of the space. According to the function of a space, the arrangement of people can be formally manipulated through a use of fixed seating, defined circulation routes and queue barriers. However, in uncluttered or small spaces people appear to organize themselves into a fascinating variety of static and moving patterns which are worth study. Stationary figures could be recorded as dots and patterns of moving individuals recorded with a line using a range of coloured pencils or pens to track a whole sequence of movements through or within each space (fig. 4).

It is a pretty good bet that your first two spaces will be rectangular in shape. The need to experience non-rectilinear space is crucial to the designer for, like the misconception of texture as a purely visual phenomenon, we can easily be conditioned into accepting the right-angle as being at the essence of man-made environment. Each designer owes it both to his own spatial education and to that of his future clients to expose himself deliberately to curvilinear space! If your immediate environment does not contain a Pantheon, a Buckminster Fuller dome, a Royal Albert Hall or a Guggenheim Museum, then you will have to use some

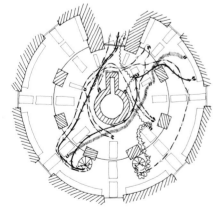

4 Movement patterns tracked in the Radcliffe Camera library, Oxford; student project.

21

ingenuity in discovering such a space. Non-rectangular interiors can be found in older buildings which often contain apses or cylindrical and domed rooms; others can be found in spaces described by spiral staircases, Victorian bandstands, circus tents or in fairgrounds and zoos.

The central aim of this exercise is to experience space through direct involvement rather than second-hand, via assumptions made from other peoples' description. The effort made in making these excursions will be rewarded by a deeper understanding of the shape, acoustics and dynamics of three different spatial types.

This study should also uncover something of the behaviour patterns of people (and yourself) using each space for it takes us towards the area of psychological research. For example, some pioneer work by E. T. Hall and R. Sommer has re-evaluated the relationship of man to his spatial setting and demonstrated that his conception of space is by no means confined to the volume occupied by his body. We exhibit similarities with animals as we carry with us various territories or bubbles of personal space which emanate from zealously guarded intimate zones and extend across private sectors to wider and less personal frontiers. Not only does this psychological space shrink and expand between personal and less exclusive parameters, but the concept of our own physical size can fluctuate in response to a psychic spatial relationship, our body seemingly growing in stature when confined in small spaces such as elevators and, conversely, diminishing within vast spaces such as cathedrals or auditoria.

The concept of non-physical space is moved to broader spectrums with K. Lewin's theory of 'psychological life-space' and the notion of 'action-space' proposed by Horton and Reynolds. Lewin's 'life-space' refers to the perceptual map in which we live out our life span. At its core is our personal space (home, room, and family) from which we journey along familiar spatial corridors for work, recreation and social contact. Extending this perceptual map are concepts of geographically distant space, its limits being electronically expanded by radio, telephone and television screen. The theory of 'action-space' attempts to relate behaviour, perception and socio-cultural attitudes. We place self-imposed limits on our location and movement through space by decisions made within socio-economic frameworks; decisions which dictate the location of our home, work and mode of travel, with additional factors such as length of residence influencing our perception of the urban environment. Such influences produce various forms of perceptual screening in different kinds of space. For instance, in a cathedral people will tend to move more slowly and speak only in whispers. In an overcrowded elevator an individual's perception of that space will be altered —just as a person experiencing a visually pleasant and thermally comfortable room 'sees' the space in a totally different fashion from someone occupying the same room with the heating increased to levels of discomfort. Kenneth Bayes has described two kinds of movements through space: '. . . one exploratory through an unknown environment the other habitual through a known environment. In the first (called 'tourist') the architecture is new, prominent and strange; one is exploring, open and receptive, moving and experiencing new things, investigating. In the second (called 'habitue') the architecture is in the background, hardly noticed; one moves through it without the awareness of the surroundings, thinking only of a goal.'[1]

However, a crucial function of this project is the experience of a non-rectilinear interior. Culturally, we live in a rectangular world —a world of space defined by buildings and boxes characterized by straight lines and right-angled corners. Even the room-space you now occupy will be created from planes, objects and openings derived from squares and rectangles which have been transferred directly from the designer's drawing-board. An over-exposure to this kind of environment has meant that, in a subtle way, our vision, being continually bombarded with rectilinear information, has developed a highly conditioned and specialized perception. A by-product of this conditioning is that our visual perception can be distorted to experience optical illusions. For example, during a visit to Jim Stirling's Olivetti Building in Surrey a group of young design students were asked to describe the plan of a roof above a ramped corridor. The majority believed that they were perceiving a parallel rectangle when, in fact, the plan was tapered (fig. 5). Optical distortions such as this are common in the perception of the modern environment

5 Camera view of ramp leading to the Reception Area seen by students visiting James Stirling's Olivetti Training Building, Haslemere, Surrey. Photo: Mike Jenks.

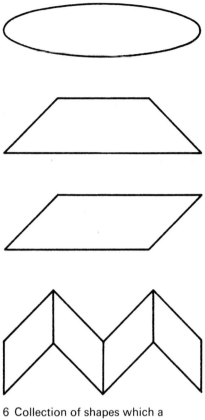

6 Collection of shapes which a conditioned visual perception refuses to interpret as being 'flat'.

7 Classic reversible figure. A perception of this image can be shifted alternately to see either two black faces or the central white vase.

such as the apparent upward thickening of tall apartment blocks and, in two dimensions, our inability to read certain shapes as being flat (fig. 6).

In comparing primitive and sophisticated perceptions the scientist, R. L. Gregory, describes the world of Zulu tribesmen who have little use for corners or straight lines. Theirs is a curvilinear culture in which dome-shaped huts filled with rounded furniture and artifacts are entered through circular openings—an agricultural society of farmers who plough, not in straight lines, but in curves. Gregory explains they do not experience the optical illusions common to our perception. Anthropologists, such as Andrew Forge, have underlined our specialized vision by demonstrating that members of the Ablam tribe in New Guinea cannot read photographs. This inability to visually translate two dimensional illusions of space is based on the fact that they have not learned to interpret photographic imagery, being much more exposed to the natural environment. In this primitive perception an environment filled with corners is an environment full of mysterious and useless adjuncts of space.

As a means of broadening your perceptual awareness it is, therefore, wise to immerse yourself consciously in spatial diversity, for our visual conditioning not only influences the formation, externalization and development of ideas but predetermines the nature of a resulting architecture, which, in turn, conditions the perceptions of those who inhabit it.

4. Conceptual Space

The design of space is, at first, a mental concept and any resultant response is primarily experienced through visual perception. However, a form-orientated approach in which space can be literally ignored or, if considered, exist as a kind of waste-product after design is still prevalent in architectural circles. It is essential, therefore, that in tuning our mental attitude to the transfer of visual information a step is made across this conceptual threshold—from a form dominated perception to a renewed awareness of space as dynamic, tangible substance. This threshold can be traversed by conducting a simple experiment using the classic figure-ground model (fig. 7).

By fixing our vision to the central vase image as object we can apprehend the traditional conception of form in space where the contours defining the vase represent form-orientated thinking the vase symbolizes an architecture of containment. However, if we psychologically switch off to a concentration on the outer areas (the two face profiles) we discover that the surrounding negative transforms into a positive but different entity which not only reflects the nature of the vase but takes on a life and meaning of its own! In our new perception, what was at first void has now become tangible—the vase to faces alternation causes a graphic experience of the concept of space as a dynamic presence, being redefined by the same contours which had previously described the vase. In returning to analogy with architecture, we can begin to understand a positive concept of environmental space in which the space between buildings is just as potent as the spaces they contain.

Project: Spatial Diagramming (interior space)
The purpose of the first of these exercises is to plot a sequence of lines between selected points in an interior space. This is not a figurative drawing, i.e., one which

24

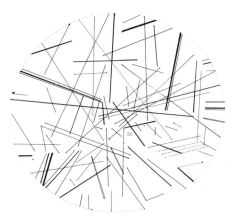

8 Linear trajectories through an interior room space; student project.

records objects, but a subjective diagram because the lines you will experience do not visually exist.

Take up a position at the edge of your chosen interior space and on a full page of a large sketchpad begin to carefully draw a single line which connects two arbitrary points in your field of vision. The initial line could, for example, connect a point on the tip of your nose to a point on the facing wall (possibly, to the corner of a piece of furniture or, if you face a window, to a point outside). A second line could join a point on the ceiling to a chosen point on the floor plane; a third moving between two horizontally or diagonally related features across your visual field —and so on. Continue selecting pairs of points of varying proximities and spatial locations using confident lines to track a trajectory between them. The subsequent build-up of the individual, criss-crossing lines should attempt to exhaust the three dimensions of the perceived space —the final diagram appearing as a complex linear structure.

The aim of this project is not to create a drawing as an end-product but to create in a diagram a thinking attitude which has transported your mind's eye through an interior space. In graphically recording the forces and tensions between physical points, the resulting skeletal structure reflects the scaffolding of a personal thinking process which has contributed to a drawing of space itself (fig. 8).

A further consideration might be the shape of the diagram. If you compare the format of your sketchbook with the outer shape of your visual field, it becomes apparent that the eye's perceptual window on the world is elliptical and not governed by the right-angle. This may be reflected in the shape of your diagram, in that your delineation of space is contained within an oval format.

Project: Spatial Diagramming (exterior space)
The second of the diagramming exercises should be made in an outdoor urban or rural corridor of space. This could be an examination of a hard-edged spatial tunnel as defined by the close proximity of man-made planes such as those found in narrow streets and alleys. The corridor effect can be discovered in older, more human-scale parts of cities where colonnades, arcades and arched, winding passages function as intimate spatial holes. Alternatively, the diagram might study the softer edges of spatial funnels created by tree-lined lanes or avenues. This sensation is readily experienced in the countryside where, along footpaths, overhanging trees together with hedges and verges tend to enclose a green and inviting tube of space.

By positioning yourself so that a view along the selected corridor is obtained, make a sketchbook diagram in pencil which, in describing a series of diminishing sections, takes your mind's eye on a sequence of linear journeys which progressively identifies the changing character of its route. These should act as conceptual cuts across selected planes along your visual path which, like the dicing of a hollow object, record the periphery of space (fig. 9). In exploring the interface between physical objects, this diagram is another version of a graphic dialogue with a developing conception of space as a dynamic entity and a subsequent diagram could record its shape through horizontal cuts.

Thus far, we have touched on several different kinds of spatial boundaries: from the psychological parameters of inter-personal space, the tactile and sound reverberating edges of physical space and the study of the visual interface between solid and void. In continuing a graphic study which focuses our visual perception

25

9 Project to determine boundaries of space seen as sections drawn at progressively distant points from the observer.

on relationships between forms rather than isolated objects, we now move to the mapping of our visual parameters.

Although we may be physically confined by the horizontal and vertical planes of a room-space, our visual boundaries can extend via its openings such as windows and open doors to spatial points beyond —even, possibly, to points on the distant horizon. Similarly, in walking through the winding streets of a hill town, our vision would alternately be restrained by its walls and, between gaps in buildings, allowed to explode into the surrounding landscape. This near/far fluctuation of the limits of our vision is the aim of this exercise which attempts to plot such parameters in a simple diagrammatic form.

Project: Diagramming Spatial Boundaries (exterior space)
Find an identifiable city, town or village space such as a cross-roads or square and, after exploring its inner, outer, and connecting spaces, make a simple sketchbook plan in pencil of the surrounding buildings and other forms which combine to form its particular degree of enclosure. Next, stand at or near the middle of the space and, by rotating on the spot, superimpose on the plan a line which describes at eye-level the shape of the limits of your all-round field of vision. Obviously, these parameters

26

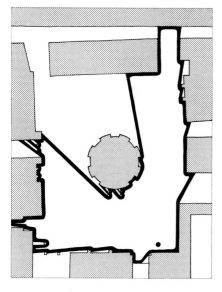

10 Diagram of a spatial boundary made at eye-level by a rotating observer.

are governed by the relative positions, directions and heights of surrounding forms relative to your revolving point of view. The line will echo the existence of these related forms within the diagram but as they are liable to suddenly shoot out between gaps to points in the far distance (and, consequently beyond the limits of your map) allow them to bleed off the edge of the sketchpad. However, the continuous line in seeking out the edges of spatial pockets will, when completing its circuit, appear as a bubble of space with your mind's eye at its centre (fig. 10).

If we compared this spatial bubble with the plan drawn in the elevator or a small room, we would immediately see a remarkable difference in their character. Similarly, if we were to make a second spatial boundary diagram only a few steps away from the first we would again experience a bubble, but vastly different. It is within this continual modification of our visual space that we can begin to identify the functioning of spatial components. For example, if we make a simple analysis of the diagram, its configuration of rays will indicate much about the visual quality of the studied space. It will communicate not only its basic character but something of its degrees of complexity and enclosure. The diagram can also indicate the relative location and size of objects together with the direction and extent of visual contact with other space beyond; its narrow shafts signifying sneak glimpses at points where the surrounding mass is punctured or wider corridors informing of more panoramic links —places where space gushes into the void outside.

From a diagram which records the parameters of our spatial experience we next move to an analytical drawing which involves a documentation of several of the spatial signals which indicate distance and depth in our perception of form.

5. Pictorial Space

Our visual experience of space relies upon a hierarchy of optical functions which are triggered by a visual contact with the real world around us. The primary visual signals or cues which aid our perception of depth are binocular vision and motion parallax.

Binocular vision can be divided into three component but related parts: accommodation, convergence and disparity. Accommodation is the ability to focus the eyes on only one point at a time. Convergence is the angle subtended by the two eyes on the object in focus —a nearer object subtending a larger angle, a more distant object a smaller angle (fig. 11). Disparity describes the fact that each eye receives a slightly different image from a perceived stimulus. These cues are signalled independently to the brain where they are integrated with all other sensory phenomena to compound a total perception.

Our eyes give overlapping fields of view and stereoscopic depth vision; motions of the head and eyes give motion parallax; so movement at right-angles to a line of vision alters the relative positions of two unequally distant objects, for example the relative movements of nearer trees and distant hills seen from a speeding train (fig. 12). Motion parallax depth information can also be perceived by a one-eyed person who, in panning like a ciné camera, would make extra use of compensatory head movements. Apart from motion pictures and stereoscopic images, all two-dimensional forms of spatial representation equate to the one-eyed person's view of space but from fixed points —monocular vision lacking the vital head movements which preclude any use of the primary cues to depth. The pictorial images created by graphic displays have to rely totally upon the secondary cues to

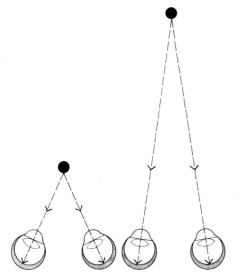

11 Convergence in depth perception. Pivoting eyes adjust to near and further objects.

27

12 Two-dimensional pictures do not change with different viewing positions. In reality, this view from a moving train would involve motion parallax, ie, that objects appear to travel at progressively decreasing speeds between foreground and background.

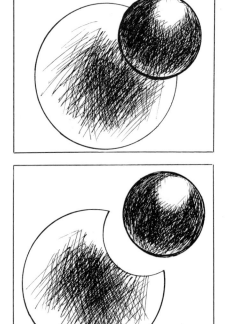

13 Illusion in the language of two-dimensions. The assumption that the small circle exists in front of the larger may be incorrect.

depth: relative apparent size (linear perspective), light and shadow, atmospheric haze (aerial perspective), and overlap.

We can study these secondary cues to depth by pursuing a very simple experiment:

(1) draw two separate but differently sized circles on a page in your sketchbook. Due to a lack of further depth cues, the larger of the two will—because of its apparent size—appear to be the nearer; existing on a plane closer to the eye. This illusion can be intensified if we shade the smaller circle darker than the larger—the apparent brightness of the larger reinforcing the illusion of its nearness.

(2) if we redraw the two circles with the smaller inside and at the centre of the larger, the resultant space becomes ambiguous—a visual conundrum caused by the lack of depth cues. Does this new image represent inner space (a microscopic view of two blood corpuscles or two atoms); interior space (a view down a tube); exterior space (a plan of a hat or a doughnut); outer space (a planet passing its sun); or non-physical space (a diagram of the Colgate 'ring of confidence')?

(3) if we again redraw the two circles but this time with the smaller partially overlapping the larger, a more powerful secondary depth cue operates which reverses the first spatial impression. The idea that a portion of the larger circle is hidden by its smaller counterpart instantly informs the eye of a new juxtaposition; the hidden area has not ceased to exist, it has simply been removed from view with the resulting implication of a certain distance existing between the two objects. In other words, our conditioned eye and brain has inferred a space which has been learned from our visual experience and recreated pictorially by overlap—the partial concealment of further by nearer forms being the most potent of the secondary cues to depth.

(4) if we assume a light source and add tonal shading to the overlapping circles we can further this illusion of depth. But even this seemingly convincing picture can be ambiguous! We can, yet again, question our perception of the apparently overlapping circles by applying a more complicated but feasible answer: that the larger circle now exists in front of the smaller—the latter being viewed precisely through a cut-away portion of the former (fig. 13). The psychologist, J. J. Gibson, employed just this visual trick in his famous experiment designed to determine the relative importance of the various depth cues. He cut away the corner of a larger, nearer playing card precisely where it 'overlapped' the view of a further, smaller playing card when perceived with one eye from a fixed position through a peephole in his viewing apparatus (fig. 14). He found that the overlap cue, even when spatially reversed, was so powerful that it negated all other secondary cues to depth. We can examine the secondary cues in a simple objective drawing.

Project: The Secondary Cues to Depth

The aim of this drawing is to translate analytically an object into differing perceptions responding to four of the secondary depth cues. It can either be worked in your sketchpad or on the drawing-board. The project also requires a separate sheet of thin paper, a pencil, pen, charcoal (or conté crayon).

Preparation; firstly, design and draw a series of horizontal black and white bands on the separate sheet of paper. When inking or painting in the black areas attempt to exploit a varying range of black and white band widths between, say, the thickness of a single pen line to one inch. Secondly, crush the completed artwork into a crumpled paper ball. Partially open up the paper into a freestanding mass of lines, form and space. You now have the source for this drawing project. Thirdly, position the crumpled paper under a strong light and, with your drawing paper and materials, position yourself so that you have a comfortable and unrestricted view of its entire configuration. Next, make a large outline drawing of the outer shape of the entire paper mass and when satisfied as to its relative proportion divide your sheet into four equal parts with a horizontal and vertical line.

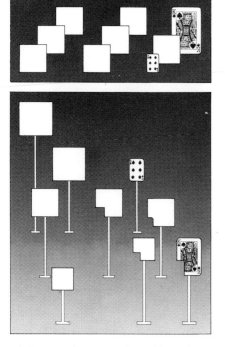

14 *Top:* cards as seen by subjects in Gibson's test; those on the left were judged as 'nearer'. *Below:* card set-up in the viewing apparatus; in fact, the right-hand cards were nearer the subjects.

(1). Relative Apparent Size (linear perspective). The first drawing concentrates purely on the distorted configuration of the black and white bands and is recorded in the top left section of your drawing-board format. Carefully outline and ink in the distorted stripe pattern as it appears from your viewpoint. As with the vase-faces figure, use a line which consciously and simultaneously describes both the black and white stripes—in other words, applying a double-checking perception which, in switching from negative (white) to positive (black) makes for a greater proportional accuracy. The transfer of the black band distortion on to the drawing-board produces a powerful illusion of depth (fig. 15). The fact that nearer portions of the band system appear to be bigger than more distant areas reflects the monocular cue of relative apparent size—relationships which convey convincing information about a spatial arrangement in a simple illusion.

A further aspect of apparent size is the relative position of objects in the visual field. For example, the higher your viewing angle to the crumpled paper, the more its nearer points will appear as lower than the higher, further points. This association of juxtaposed forms with distance is another depth cue related to a

15 Depth illusion in the relative size of black and white stripes.

perceptual stance in which more distant objects appear as more elevated in relation to the viewer's position in space. Although many primitive and traditional perceptions do not always connotate size fluctuation with depth in pictorial depiction, they do utilize the relative positioning of objects on the picture plane. In oriental painting, objects and figures can, without any size modifications, be placed at various heights on the picture plane to convey a strong sense of space.

(2). Light and Shadow. Moving to the lower-left sector of the analysis, concentrate on the physical structure and surface of the paper mass. Try to explore the spatial quality of light using charcoal or conté crayon to extract and analyse the precise shape and tone of shadow patterns. In assessing the contrast between light and shade it is useful to half-close the eyes for this tends to filter out extraneous information which might confuse the analysis.

Again, we have focused upon a potent clue to depth for shadows indicate the strength and direction of light, the relative positions of overhanging features and reveal both the profiles and, depending on the degree of sensitivity in tone application, the surface texture of form. Also, within this section of the drawing shadows cast from the crumpled paper onto its support could be included as a means of indicating its outer mass.

(3). Atmospheric Haze (aerial perspective). In this quarter of the drawing (being worked in the top-right section) tune-in to the paper surface, band system and background space, to investigate the role played by atmospheric haze in two-dimensional illusions. This depth cue refers to the perceived greater clarity of nearer points in space in contrast with those more distant. It was Leonardo da Vinci who first discussed this depth-effect in terms of painting when he noticed differences in colour between points in space; particles in the atmosphere causing further objects

30

to appear lighter and less clearly defined than objects near at hand. This project involves a stretching of the tonal scale from sharper, darker frontal tones to lighter variations in the background. This can be achieved by the introduction of a system of dots drawn in pencil or pen which being constructed more tightly in the foreground areas, progress through a scale to looser systems which describe the space beyond the paper mass. This 'pointilliste' technique, being originally influenced by printing processes, shows how our eye and brain can construct depth images. For example, if we closely examine a newspaper photograph we find it is comprised of black ink dots on a white ground. In moving away the dots are quickly assembled by the eye into a tonal pattern which is interpreted by the brain as an identifiable image communicating an illusion of depth.

(4). Overlap. The fourth depth cue to investigate is overlap. Using a pen or pencil line, progressively describe the contours of the paper masses as each partially blocks off the view of the one behind until a spatial sequence of overlap is established. This linear sequence could be extended to any objects lying behind and beyond the source object. A use of thicker, darker lines on nearer forms and thinner, lighter lines on background forms will intensify the overlap illusion.

On completing this drawing we can compare the characteristics of these four depth cues in conveying illusions of depth but, in doing so, we should consider some further aspects of illusion-making on a flat plane. For example, the very surface texture of your drawing paper can countermand the effect of the depth cues by informing the eye that the surface is flat. This accounts for the highly polished finish of *trompe l'oeil* and Super-Realist paintings which to achieve an almost photographic illusion of reality rely upon both a powerful exploitation of the secondary depth cues and a meticulously flat surface. However, these illusions only occur as long as the pictorial image is beyond the distance where binocular vision is effective and there is no movement away from a fixed point. This can be demonstrated by viewing your drawing from one side —by moving your viewing position away from the fixed viewpoint any illusion created by your drawing is destroyed and distorted.

A further factor must also be accounted for if our representation of space is to be congruent with our perception of reality —the phenomenon of constancy, the difference between the image which enters the eye and the image reconstructed by the brain. This phenomenon refers to a zoom-lens capacity of the brain which compensates for the shrinkage of objects with distance. It can be illustrated by the appearance of an audience from a theatre stage; all the faces in the auditorium will look much the same size and yet the retinal image of the nearest faces are far larger than those at the back. In viewing photographs or measured perspective drawings, constancy scaling does not readily occur. This is because the camera and the mechanical rules of perspective reproduce the retinal image and not the brain's picture (fig. 16). Artists overcome this problem to some extent by bending the laws of perspective and draw what they see rather than recreate the retinal image (fig. 17).

The secondary cues studied in our drawing also contribute to our perception of real space but only in so far as they enhance or deny spatial meaning obtained by binocular vision. In qualifying binocular depth information they can create illusions

16 Photographic image does not account for constancy scaling and foreshortening distortion results. Reproduced by permission of Department for National Savings (who wish to point out that these certificates are no longer on sale).

31

a

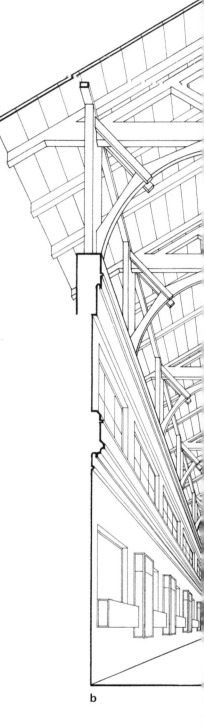

b

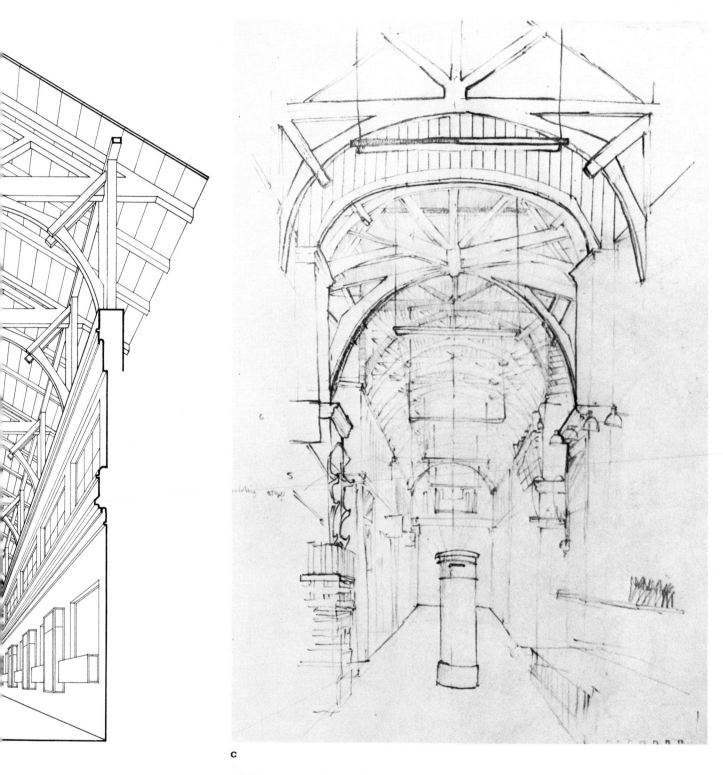

c

17 Three perceptions of Oxford's covered market: (a) 'retinal image' of a camera;
(b) 'retinal image' of a constructed perspective; (c) modified eye and brain
image of a freehand sketch—note the effect of constancy scaling which
establishes the back wall plane as existing nearer the observer. Photo: Mike
Jenks.

33

18 David Hockney, *Kirby (After Hogarth) Useful Knowledge*, 1975. Oil on canvas, 72 × 60⅛ in. Collection, The Museum of Modern Art, New York. Purchase and gift of the artist and J. Kasmin.

Notes
[1] Bayes, K. *The Therapeutic Effect of Environment on Emotionally Disturbed and Mentally Subnormal Children* Unwin, London, 1967.

and abiguities which have been pictorially exploited in both a serious and humorous fashion by such artists as Hogarth, Escher, Albers and Hockney (fig. 18).

In converting two-dimensional messages into three-dimensional meanings, our brain seems to reconstruct space by taking into consideration distance and depth. Space without content, however, is meaningless; space is defined by objects which act as sensory agents—each having perceptual properties of their own such as size, shape, surface and form. To extend our dialogue with experience, we now turn to a consideration of these elements.

34

3   The Spatial Elements

'Variety is not only the spice of life, it is the very stuff of it.'
J. Vernon

Part of our legacy from the Renaissance is a notion of form and volume as defined by the visual elements —line, shape, colour, texture and form. Most present-day design courses are founded on this principle, whose fundementals were re-expounded afresh in the Bauhaus by teachers including Johannes Itten, Paul Klee and Wassily Kandinsky. Their educational philosophy, examining the spatial experience and co-ordination of design from fundamentals, has contributed a great deal to the designers' understanding of the potential of formal arrangement. However, a fragmentation in spatial analysis, however unavoidable, can lead to a schismatic approach to evironmental design, an attitude which isolates consideration of the interaction of form and void from its interface—the surface elements.

A glimpse over the architect's shoulder finds his graphic representation of space usually drawn or rendered in black and white: even small-scale models are constructed with a greater concern for achromatic plastic qualities than for manipulation of the wider range of controlling elements. By comparison, our real perception of space is subject to a wholistic process, an integrated faculty in which each spatial variable is experienced in context together with all the others, as in a kaleidoscope. To take one example, our perception of colour is constantly and simultaneously modified by a supplementary experience of texture and form; in other words, colour is texture and form. We experience each of the spatial elements as a component of all the others.

The projects contained in this chapter are, therefore, intended to heighten awareness of these elements, both in our perception of them and their subsequent articulation on the drawing-board.

Project: Shape, Rhythm and Line
Materials: pencils, pens, and a large sheet of paper.
Stage One: select an outer frame for this exercise different from the traditional square or rectangle; choose, say, a circle, triangle or diamond. In pencil, draw the selected format as large as possible on the paper and divide the shape into three equal areas which will act as sectors for three families of shapes. In the first sector draw the pencil outline of a whole sequence of shapes derived from the circle, in the second, a variety of shapes which relate to the square and, finally, an extensive range of doodled, free-form shapes in the third.

The potential variety of size and shape should be exploited within each family and characteristic differences exploited between each sector. The outlines of the circular and square shapes could be constructed but the free-form shapes should be freely drawn. In each case, make sure that none of the shapes contained within the complete field overlap those of any other.

Stage Two: having filled each sector with its respective collection of shapes, begin to explore the left-over spaces between the shapes with an ink line which, in responding to the outline character of different shapes, moves on an exploratory walk through the three fields. A series of such journeys could be made; some lines beginning at the outer frame and working inwards, either terminating at an arbitrary point inside the field or, starting inside the frame and, after wandering between various sectors, forming its own shape by connecting back with its starting point. This investigation of two-dimensional space could utilize a variety of line thickness—sensuous and delicate in more gentle rhythms and stronger, more robust along more direct routes (fig. 1).

The project can be worked on from all sides of its frame, either by moving around it or turning the sheet of paper. This is also true of the finished design for, having no obvious 'top' and 'bottom', the shaped field can be viewed in any position.

The object of this exercise is to experience the wealth of diversity of shape and line, their interaction creating a complex linear rhythm which, as we rotate the drawing into different viewing positions, provides a changing stimulus for our emotions. Maurice de Sausmarez tells us that the line signifies directional energy capable of bearing emotional connotations which can convey aggression when thickened and stability when straight. This is, to an extent, borne out by psychological studies such as the ones cited by P. F. Smith, which have apparently found a scale of emotional ups and downs equating to the rise and fall of lines. Upward curves elicit a sense of cheerfulness while their descending counterparts register a corresponding emotional slump. When the stability of a straight line loses control, its zig-zag pulsation assumes such an emotional electricity that it has attracted both the attentions of psychologists and more scientific artists such as Vasarely (fig. 2).

A zig-zag linear decoration was also highly popular in primitive design and, on tracing its journey through architectural time and space its pulsating rhythm—after its primitive cavorting—was harnessed to a structure of harmonic, gilded

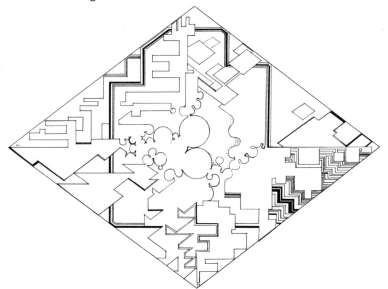

1 Series of linear 'walks' around fields of circles, rectangles, parallelograms and triangles contained within a parent diamond.

proportion upon which to hang the flesh of ancient concepts of space. The Gothic builder ordered the line to skyrocket, then the Renaissance commanded it to chase Brunelleschi's vanishing dot through horizontal layers of ordered space and into infinity. After its adolescence —scribbling its way around the delights of Baroque confectionery—its rhythmic pulse began a gradual descent into a premature senility, occasionally flickering with excitement in the minds of more creative designers. Until exposed by modern painters, a linear scaffolding had lurked between canvas and paint, whose ambiguities Albers examined and which escaped from the confines of the picture plane and spread, via De Stijl and Constructivist drawing-boards, into the built environment. Set against its more recent and spectacular performances in the stimulation-seeking eyes of Op artists the line on the contemporary drawing-board seems bent on right-angles, seemingly responding to Mondrian's vision of a spatial world in complete submission to the grid. However, at its worst, this kind of vision finds a response in the appearance of more lines —of dissent sprayed from the aerosol cans of the phantom graffiti artist!

Whenever we connect the two ends of a line (as in the project), the contained

2 Victor Vasarely, *Zint*, 1952–60. Oil on canvas, 108 × 100 cm. Courtesy of the artist.

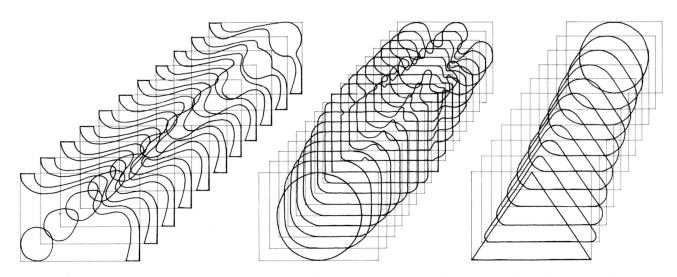

3 Metamorphic development of a freeform separating in two, a circle into a freeform, and a triangle into a circle.

area assumes a concept of shape perceptually detached from the surrounding area; this figure-ground phenomenon relegates the line into subserviency. Our experience of the potential diversity of shape can be extended through a series of metamorphic exercises, a sequence of stages in the gradual transformation of shapes between one family and another, for example, between a square and a circle and on into a pre-designed free-form (fig. 3).

The purpose of this study is the development of an analytical view of architecture, a critical perception which filters architectural mass into components of shape, line and rhythm, observing directional linear patterns, skylines and repeated elements such as columns, windows, doors and arches. By employing this mental undressing technique we move towards an understanding of scale and proportion. However, the architectural elements of line, shape and mass have, as part of their spatial characteristics, surface quality. Every building material has a surface colour and texture. As such, they are governed by the same laws that apply to the other spatial elements but, unfortunately, surface colour and texture appear to occur in our built environment more by accident than by design. For this reason, we should first understand why it is that we are fortunate enough to be endowed with the faculty of colour vision.

The first answers to this question can be found in the work of the zoologist, Nicholas Humphrey, who suggests that man's evolution of colour vision is intimately linked to the evolution of colour on the surface of the Earth. In a world without colour, what use would colour vision be! Even before colour vision evolved, some living tissues were already coloured —blood was 'red' and foliage 'green'. However, the most striking colours of nature, those found in flowers, birds and fish were all evolutionary creations deliberately developed to act as visual signals, carrying messages to those eyes equipped to perceive them. Humphrey speculates that the early tree-dwelling primates later moved in on an ecological niche previously occupied by birds who could already see colour. In order to survive, to compete effectively with birds, primates needed to evolve colour vision. The later emergence of man, however, developed this part of the evolutionary survival kit into a new skill (shared only by the Bower Bird and the aesthetic chimpanzee) —the ability to apply colour where it does not naturally occur. The first steps in developing this ability are the concern of the next project.

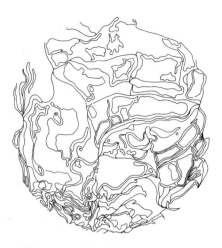

4 Linear map of colour change seen through a circular viewfinder on the surface of a cabbage.

Project: Mapping a Colour Perception (Colour Analysis)
Materials: one sheet of paper (minimum size 33 by 24 inches), brushes, pencils, and a range of gouache including a red, blue, yellow, purple, black and white.

Remove a page from your sketchbook and, from its middle, cut a small circular hole two inches in diameter. The hole now becomes a window through which we embark on a search for colour. Select a subject for a colour analysis such as that of a variegated apple or any fruit, a cake or, indeed, any surface which you find stimulating in colour (for the purposes of this exercise even a coloured magazine photograph would suffice). Next, move the paper window over the surface of your chosen subject until an area interesting in colour relationships is isolated. In the case of the coloured photograph, however, avoid framing identifiable images such as a hand or a face —recognition of which might, in the analysis, contaminate a concentrated study of abstract colour.

Stage One: draw the equivalent of your circular window in pencil on the sheet of cartridge, increasing its diameter to eighteen inches. By viewing the source area through the paper window directly applied to the object, transfer in line the shapes of colour one by one, enlarging them into an accurate structure in the drawing (fig. 4). Try to describe meticulously the character of each shape until the linear structure is complete. Obviously, the more concentrated your perception, the wider your spectrum of colour experience —it is the extension of this experience which is the central aim of the project.

Stage Two: then, matching each colour by careful observation of your source paint each of the shapes. Mix each colour to a sufficient consistency to be an opaque layer —each colour-patch making contact with its neighbours and thereby obliterating all evidence of the pencil lines. Should you discover that the basic range of paint cannot cope with the demands of your perception, use additional colours, but only after the collapse of exhaustive colour-mixing experiments. Any surplus pigment left on the brush after each application could be introduced into a list of colours at the side of the sheet —a schematic colour ladder registering your number of colour discriminations (fig. 5).

During the analysis, a whole series of changes in colour impressions may occur, change due to natural light shifts or the slow deterioration of the source object, changes due to near and far viewing distances and in wet and dry pigment and change in colour interaction, i.e., the appearance of a colour, first against white paper and then in context with other colours. The world of colour is quite remarkable, a world of changing impressions made up of speckles and patches within, even, the tiny window used in our study. This and subsequent investigations will, hopefully, work against the casual glance at an object which informs us that, for instance, grass is 'green' or a brick 'red'. Such cursory impressions are only formed because we have learned, through colour constancy, to project back from our mind a colour we normally associate with an object.

However, the colours we see do not exist on the surface of substance, for they are manufactured in the mind's eye. Our experience of colour is a subjective sensation conveyed through the energy in wavelength form of light radiations within the visible spectrum. However, without an observer, light rays do not, in themselves, constitute colour. As Sir Isaac Newton explained in his *Optiks*, 'The rays are not coloured. In them there is nothing else than a power to stir up a sensation of this or

39

5 Student colour analysis of a section from a magazine photograph. The steps of the accompanying colour ladder document the number of mixes involved, ie, the number of different colours perceived.

that colour.' The eye and brain of the observer interprets the meaning of these sensory messages; the resultant colour perception depends on three important factors. First, the conditions under which our object was viewed: for example, certain colours painted under tungsten light would appear very different from those painted in natural sunlight, as the two colour perceptions respond to two different spectral energy distributions contained in each light source. Second, a colour perception depends on the spectral characteristics of the object, the ability of its substance to absorb, reflect or transmit light. Red paint, for instance, appears as red because it has the property of absorbing from white light everything except the red component of the light. The third factor is our ability to perceive colours, i.e., the sensitivity of our colour-making mechanism (the eye and brain) to create a colour response.

40

In reaching the eyes, sensory messages of wavelength are decoded by light-sensitive nerve cells located in the retina and known as rods which give a perception of white, grey and black. Also located in the retina are around fifty thousand colour receptors known as cones. In a colour response they are fired by light wavelengths of red, green, and blue, and convey messages along the optic nerve for their ultimate experience in the visual projection region of the brain. The idea that colour is seen in the brain is, therefore, correct in this sense for we can experience colour with our eyes shut as in dreams. The existence of our personal Technicolor processing laboratory is further exampled in the incidence of anomalous colour vision, popularly mis-called colour-blindness, due to one or more sets of cones either mis-firing or being completely out of action.

The mechanics of colour vision, however, are an extensive and exciting study: the books for a more thorough investigation are listed in the bibliography.

Project: A Colour Experiment
Draw a circle in pencil approximately ten inches in diameter on a sheet of cartridge paper. Around its circumference, equidistant from each other, place four one inch diameter circles, the first at the top. Next, paint the left-hand circle red.
Experiment (a): after concentrating your gaze on the red disc for several seconds, transfer it to the blank circle situated diametrically opposite. In doing so, you should experience a new colour sensation. The resulting mirage of a bluish-green is called a negative after-image and is thought to be caused by the previous over-stimulation of the red-sensitive cones which, when the stimulus is removed, triggers an involuntary firing of the green. The old saying that 'red and green should never be seen' refers to this opposition for they are known as complementary colours. This double-acting perception forms the basis of the Hering Opponent-Colour Theory which postulates that there are three pairs of processes in the eye, each consisting of two opposite colours (red-green, blue-yellow and white-black). Such after-images can be found on a large scale. For example in a pharmaceutical factory production-line workers began to complain of seeing greenish spots before their eyes. The problem was solved by placing green coloured screens in the work area, as the spots had been caused by the effect of concentratedly checking purple-red pills.

After painting the right-hand disc green, colour the top in yellow and, after experiencing the mirage of its negative after-image in the lower circle, paint in the appropriate colour. In doing so, a basic version of Newton's colour circle is established; a colour wheel he formed by bending the spectrum (fig. 6). The wheel contains the three primary colours (red, yellow and blue) together with a green (although green is not strictly a primary colour as it can be mixed from blue and yellow, owing to its psychological content it achieves such status in several colour systems). Locate four more small circles around the wheel each positioned between the existing colour discs. After painting them in equal admixtures derived from the colours of their neighbours, we establish intermediate or secondary colours. The resultant colour circle represents the basic families of colour, the first of the three dimensions of colour—hue. Hue is that quality which is commonly accepted as colour in defining its redness, blueness or yellowness.
Experiment (b): draw a chain of five, one inch circles diametrically connecting the red and green disc. Paint the small circle next to the red disc in an admixture of four-

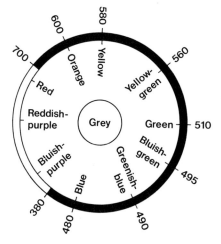

6 The colour circle, showing the principal hues and their position around its perimeter. The numbers, in nanometres, indicate wavelengths of light corresponding to the hues.

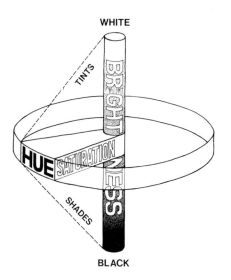

7 Three-dimensional colour space. This diagram illustrates the relationships between hue, saturation (chroma), and brightness (value).

parts red to one of green; in the next, three-parts red to two of green. Also, work inwards from the green disc through similar proportionate mixtures but, this time, with increasing additions of red pigment—in two progressive stages—modifying the green. Finally, in the centre circle paint a fifty-fifty mix of red and green. This new scale of colour represents the second colour dimension—saturation (or chroma). This is a distinguishing factor which relates to the chromatic strength of a colour impression. For example, the intensity of the red and green disc has been progressively reduced or desaturated by the increasing addition of the other until both submit to an achromatic or muddy grey at the centre.

Imagine that the red, blue and green discs are torches (flashlights) which beam their respective shafts of light to a meeting point on the ceiling, the coloured lights would mix additively to create a white. The reason why the yellow torch was not switched on for our conceptual model is because, in using coloured light, we employ an *additive* colour mixture as distinct from the *subtractive* colour in our painting. From combinations of red, green and blue light it is possible to make nearly all the colours; this process being used for colour film and television. Imagine also that, below the colour wheel is another point—a second pole in opposition to the white which, in representing black, terminates a descending scale of increasingly darkening colour shadows. We have, in fact, conceptualized two cones, one above and one below our colour circle. If we now, in the mind's eye, allow this figure to move upwards and position itself in front of us with its black pole standing on the drawing-board—we have a close encounter of the third kind of colour dimension (fig. 7). This vertical scale is the way we can distinguish colour in terms of brightness (or value), which roughly corresponds to the amount of physical energy or intensity of light, i.e., the lightness or darkness of a colour.

This conceptual model basically represents the world of colour; a world which has had its three dimensions and, therefore, its shape modified by a whole series of colour theories. After Newton's initial mapping of its equator in 1660, its geography has been classified and re-annotated by a series of systems, namely those by H. Lambert (1772), M. E. Chevreul (1861), A. H. Munsell (1898), W. Ostwald (1915), and in 1976, by A. Hård (fig. 8).

Psycho-physiological research has found that reactions to colour through the eye (and skin) are many, varied and intriguing. For example, the researcher, Kurt Goldstein, wrote: 'It is probably not a false statement if we say that a specific colour stimulation is accompanied by a specific response pattern in the entire organism.'[1] In summarizing his work, he suggests that the perception of colour affects muscular tension, brain waves, heart rate, respiration and other functions of the autonomic nervous system, and certainly it aroused definite emotional and aesthetic responses. However, the speculation and myth surrounding the meanings we associate with colour paints a confusing picture. Yellow, for instance, has been suggested as a good colour for libraries and classrooms as it was thought to stimulate the intellect, but art therapists have observed that suicidally inclined patients tend to use yellow pigment generously in their painting—as, indeed, did Van Gogh. Red is also seen as a powerful, active colour while green, on the other hand, has traditionally been thought of as calming. On this basis it was employed by the last governor of Alcatraz when he used a green for the redecoration of the solitary confinement areas in an attempt to pacify his involuntary guests. Blue is seen as a cool, lightweight and recessive colour and is

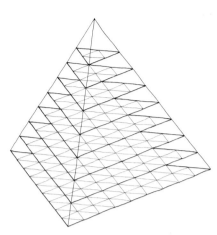

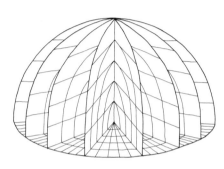

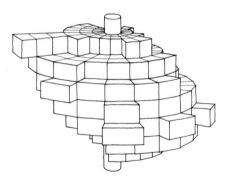

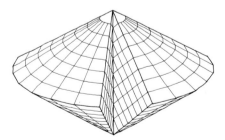

8 Series of annotated conceptual colour solids representing the theories of H. Lambert, M. E. Chevreul, A. H. Munsell, and W. Ostwald.

less-clearly focused on the eye than the so-called warmer and heavier red-based hues. This spatial effect was first noted by Leonardo da Vinci and subsequent generations of painters who have understood that different areas of coloured paint can occupy different apparent positions in space.

Meanwhile, some recent research by the Swedish psychologist, Lars Sivik, challenges some of the common attributes we associate with colours. He claims that most colour experiments are limited by their confinement to the laboratory and, using new techniques in measuring colour judgements, Sivik conducted his experiments outside. The importance of the three colour dimensions of hue, saturation (chroma) and brightness (value) are central to his findings on the meanings we associate with colour. His exhaustive investigations question, for example, the common idea that green colours have a calming effect. He found that people do not consider a red to be more active or stimulating than a green or, indeed, any other hue —so long as the colours viewed are of equal saturation and brightness. In all his tests he discovered that the dimensions of hue, i.e., the greenness, redness, or yellowness of a colour, was much less important in environmental colour than saturation or brightness. For example, all dark colours (shades) were seen as being more masculine, more unusual and heavier than light colours (tints) and that the shades tend to reduce and clearly define space when judged in comparison with their tinted counterparts. Tints, on the other hand, were judged as being more friendly, more cultured and more pleasant, and also rated as appearing more beautiful than the darker shades.

In the context of colour temperature, Sivik's findings support the traditional belief that red appears warm and blue cold, except that a blue-red was judged as being as visually cool as the blues and blue-greens. However, Sivik underlines the importance of contextual reference and the interaction of colour and surface texture when posing the following question: 'Which of the two appear warmer —an ice-blue woollen sock or a red plastic bag?'[2]

Project: Texture and Colour Gradients
(materials required: sketchbook and coloured pencils)
As a subject for this exercise, try to find a connecting vertical and horizontal plane in the urban environment which comprises of a surface rich in texture and diversity of building materials. Finding such a source may mean a visit to an older quarter of the town or, even, a journey to a country village. Make a detailed drawing of a section of the related wallscape and floorscape planes. The drawing could be worked lengthways in the sketchbook, with the vertical surface recorded on the top page and its corresponding floorplane drawn on the bottom page —the spine functioning as a horizontal division between the two.

Through a sensitive and subtle use of colour, aim to record objectively these polychromatic and textural relationships. This will be a dynamic impression as surfaces are continually subject to modification by light which, in casting shadow pockets across textural grain, causes a detectable desaturation of its colour. Further colour-texture modifications are also effected by the softening process of parasitic growths —mosses and lichens which occur on more unused surfaces, evidence of natural reclamation.

View the completed drawing by forming a horizontal and vertical plane with the two pages of the sketchbook; positioning the lower page (floorscape drawing) at

9 Various texture gradients further intensify the illusion of depth on shapes which, in a conditioned perception, already occupy spatial planes.

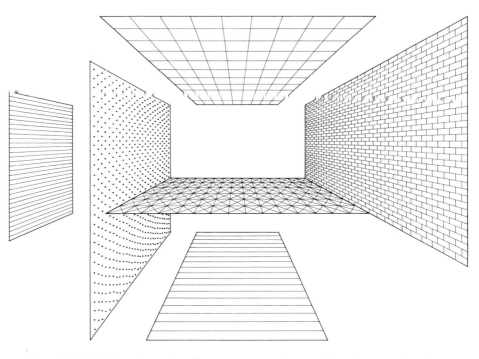

eye-level. By looking along the floorspace section at the wallscape drawing, we begin to see why surface elaboration is such a powerful cue in our perception of three-dimensional space. It is the diminishing gradient of textural pattern which intensifies a sensation of linear perspective—an effect which psychologists such as J. J. Gibson find such an important facet of our spatial understanding (fig. 9).

Texture and colour play an important role in the environment at large for, in their modulation of surface, they signal scale and depth. They can also define zones of territorial space by communicating go and no-go areas. For example, in Oxford's medieval backstreets, variegated surface treatments not only accentuate the gentle horizontal and vertical undulation of forms, but subtly demarcate individual facades and transitional zones between public and private (fig. 10). Similarly, in Greece the annual ritual of colour-washing village houses and pavements reflects a redefinition of the close working relationship of interpersonal spaces—the progressive build-up of decorative pigment softening the corners of forms and 'welding' vertical to horizontal (fig. 11). In the North of England, it is common to find the textural patterning of terraced-house brickwork re-emphasized through a meticulous application of contrasting colours. It is also on these houses that we find the 'bi-coloured downspout phenomenon'—each side of boundary drain-pipes painted in the emblematic colours of joint ownership!

By contrast, the designers of the modern environment over-indulge the polish of a machine aesthetic. This predilection for shiny surface is epitomized in a Miesian gloss which erased the embossed words 'Bethlehem Steel' from the metal of his Farnsworth glass house! Whatever light relief is provided by the architect who prints his setting concrete with wood-grain textures and the landscape designer who surfaces new town pedestrian routes with a textured, directional paving for residents who find it difficult to find their way home—we are a far cry from the surface delights of Gaudi's scintillating porcelain mosaics and the feathery shingles of Herb Greene (fig. 12).

44

The psychologist, Sven Hesselgren, has outlined three dimensions of touch. The first is the actual sensation of physical contact with the surface of an object, the moving backwards and forwards of the finger or hand at the point of contact. Hesselgren cites the studies of E. H. Webber who demonstrated that if the hand or finger-tips did not move, it was difficult to distinguish between one texture and another. The second dimension can be experienced as we pick up an object —such as an ink bottle. In holding the object we gain an immediate impression of its weight —this tactile sensation being recorded by the kinesthetic activity of our muscles which make infinitesimal adjustments to the balance of our body in space. If we now close our eyes and, using the hands, explore the entire surface of the object, we experience a third dimension of touch —a haptic perception of its form. This sensation is the most reliable of our sense organs in acquiring knowledge of the existence of a physical form—feeling is believing!

Further studies along the scales of surface sensation could be made through the compilation of a tactile reference dictionary. This could be assembled over a period of time and, by incorporating trays of found or invented textures, be ultimately affixed to a wall together with an invitation to intensify tactile perception through finger and hand contact. Each of its sections could explore the widest possible spectrum of tactile experience. Degrees of textural grain might span a range of

10 *Below left*
Wall and floorscape textures in Bath Place, Oxford; tactile signals which communicate zones of private, semi-private and public territories. Photo: Mike Jenks.

11 *Below right*
Decorative use of lime wash on vertical and horizontal surfaces in a Greek island village. Courtesy D. Vassiliadis (reproduced from *Wayfaring Across the Forms and Countenances of Greek Space*, Athens, 1976).

12 Shingles on Herb Greene's Prairie Chicken House, Norman, Oklahoma. Photo: Dan Thomas.

roughness and smoothness; a temperature scale might range from the warmth of polystyrene to the chill of steel; degrees of plasticity might be investigated from hard to elastic together with experimental scales of pleasure and pain, or security and danger. In developing ideas for the latter, one devious student made an assemblage of touch-pads from varieties of thickness and intensities of pink foam-rubber. However, participants in his display found that their initial sensations of pleasure were suddenly replaced by pain, for he had secreted several rows of sharp pins immediately below the surface!

However, architecture is not experienced exclusively by our finger-tips but by our feet and, indeed, the whole of our bodies. For instance, the ergonomic architecture of the chair takes us through a wide range of bodily sensation. Compare the hard, ungiving wooden planes of Reitveld's Red-Blue Chair against the elasticated membrane of Archizoom's triangulation, or the cold, pneumatic softness of Quasar's plastic bubbles. Again, compare the kinesthetic feel of the swivelling luxury of the Eames leather-lined barber chair with the suspension of a common, but ingenious, deck-chair, or the warmth of a beanbag against the icy austerity of Pel's plexiglass and the rigid formality of a church pew (fig. 13). Such

46

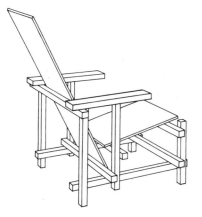
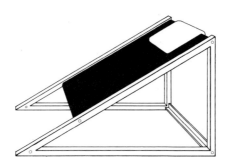
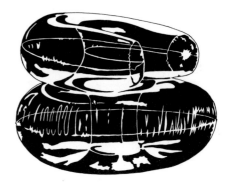

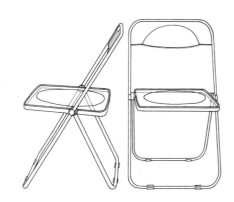

13 Various body sensations offered by chair ergonomics: red-blue chair, 'Mies' chair, Quasar Khann chair, Eames chair and ottoman, deckchair, beanbag, Plia chair and church pew.

47

sensory excursions into diversity should not be confined to a second-hand experience —such as reading —but gained from direct contact; the nature of tactile perception being heightened by the thrill of a contrasing physical contact with form.

Project: Analytical Drawing (Form, Structure and Scale)
Materials required: two sheets of paper (minimum size 33 by 24 inches) with pencils and pens. Select one of the following objects: an umbrella, an adjustable spanner or wrench, a lipstick, or a pair of spectacles.
Stage One: set up the object under reasonable illumination and position yourself in relation to it so that a representative view of its form is achieved. Make a large drawing at the centre of the first sheet which attempts to portray the formal, three-dimensional and surface characteristics of its image. Make a conscious effort to model its form through light and shade together with concentrating on a synthesis of the other depth cues. In your isolation of the source-object in the middle of the sheet, attempt to endow it with presence, as if the completed image will be used as a poster to advertise the object.
Stage Two: on the second sheet, make a series of drawings which aim to communicate the mechanical aspects of the object, i.e., a graphic explanation of its working parts, its joints, and quality, surface and connection differences in its use of materials, as if the drawing will be used to inform a person who has never before encountered such an object.

Now compare the drawings on the two sheets of paper. They should be totally different in impression, for they represent two functions of drawing. The first is simply an objective record taken from one view of its outward appearance, while the second set of drawings are dynamic (using a series of viewpoints), diagrammatic, and analytically complete. A study of the external, mechanical, and internal properties of forms should be developed in the sketchbook, a series of drawings of different attitude which search for variety in form and structure. For instance, graphic collections (possibly functioning as a private reference library) could be compiled from a study of the outward appearance of contrasting objects such as bones, stones, fruit, seedcases (like poppy-heads), and mechanisms such as plugs, bicycles and typewriters, (fig. 14). Analytical drawings of structural components could be investigated through dismantling, slicing or, employing an 'x-ray' or exploded vision which penetrates the skin of form (fig. 15). Collections of mechanical architectural form could also be gathered; kinetic structures such as telescopic gasometers, swinging bridges and rotating cranes —the library being extended by varieties of city forms such as chimneys, sculpture, monuments and towers. It is interesting to note at this point, that the Finnish architect, Reimä Pietilä described his design process as being triggered by the exclusive study of organic matter found on his wanderings in the countryside and along coastlines. After making analytical drawings from his store of objects, he then transposed them into embryonic concepts of buildings. These were then filed in his sketchbook until the moment arrived when they could be utilized in an actual design programme.

Further sketchbook studies could examine methods of connection between various building materials: some studies of skeletal building structures in the process of construction —others schematically describing the previously experienced cells of space contained within a building. The search for inner structure is

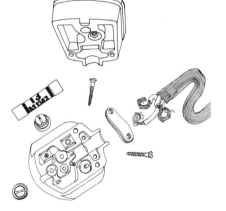

14 Student analysis of the mechanics of an electric plug.

48

15 Structural sculpture of a cabbage explored and isolated in an objective student drawing.

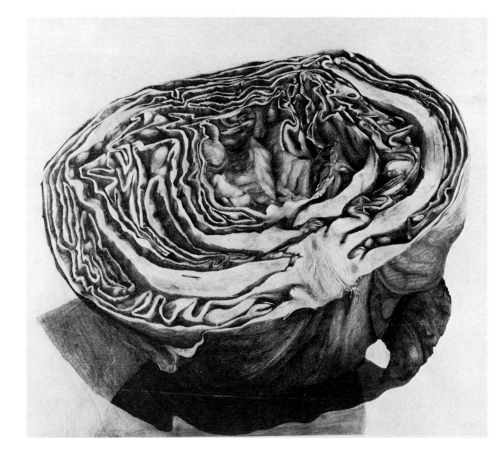

reflected in the work of the Cubists and, more dynamically, in the paintings and sculpture of the Futurists who, to parallel advances in modern physics, shifted their attentions from the outward appearance of form to its underlying structural geometry, a design approach replicated in the philosophies of many contemporary architects who claim to conceive habitable space from inside-out.

Stage Three: requirements —Imagination!

If we compare the first, objective drawing with the source-object, we will notice that the scale of the latter is governed both by your physical relationship to it and the objects which surround it. However, the drawing (which might, depending on your choice of object, be larger or smaller in physical dimension on the paper) has no inherent scale for it relates only to the blank context of its white surround. The final phase of this project, therefore, takes place in Lilliput. Allow, for example, the drawn object to grow conceptually into enormous proportions and, retaining this new conception of its scale, graphically relate it to an imaginary environmental setting. In order to establish its new scale, it could be pictorially sited on the bank of a river or lake, adorn the front of an imposing building or function as the gigantic focal point in a city square. Human figures could also be introduced who, by comparison with the object, intensify the scale of its surrounding space.

Similar games with architectural scale have also been played in the creative imagination of the sculptor, Claes Oldenburg —whose work has obviously influenced this phase of the project. Much of his inventive reversal of scale has resulted from the siting of colossal versions of everyday forms in popular city

49

spaces—some already realized through his sculpture. His London projects, for example, proposed the installation of a giant ball-cock on the Thames —a humorous landmark which would rise and fall with the tides. Others replaced Nelson's Column with a car rear-view mirror and removed Eros from Piccadilly Circus to make way for a massive lipstick (fig. 16). The humour of his Pop Art vision of American architectural form has, amongst others, dreamed up binocular buildings, hyperdermic skyscrapers, and a stock exchange edifice encased in a giant corset. There are examples in modern architecture of this *Alice in Wonderland* effect. For example, V. Tatlin's leaning Helter-Skelter, H. Greene's 'chicken', J. Utzon's sails, B. Fuller's umbrellas and Skidmore, Owings and Merrills' siting of a giant concrete doughnut in Washington's Mall (fig. 17). Such architecture can take on a little warmth and humour but also counterpoint the fact that such human responses are not always intended within the icy strictures of a pervading modernist philosophy.

In designing for the built milieu the architect, rather like an organist, can manipulate the scales and rhythms of his spatial keyboard; through pulling and depressing his design stops he can also control the volume and variety of its variables. However, the orchestration of a built environment created by many apparently tone-deaf architects makes for pervading monotony which borrows little from any real articulation of the spatial elements. By comparison, sensory deprivation experiments such as those conducted in the fifties by D. O. Hebb at McGill University, demonstrate that withdrawal of stimulation can be just as injurious to the human organism as the opposite effects of overkill. In proposing a theory to account for deprivation J. A. Vernon states, 'The human cannot long endure a homogeneous situation no matter how good and desirable it is.'[3] Another researcher, E. Miller, has said that the brain needs constantly varying forms of stimulation in order to operate. As a result of this and later work, we begin

16 Claes Oldenburg, *Lipstick in Piccadilly Circus, London*. Postcard photomontage, 1966. Courtesy The Tate Gallery.

50

to understand that the human organism and its nervous system actually seek a contrasting sensory stimulation which is only rarely provided for in the mainstream architecture illustrated in glossy magazines.

In order to understand more fully this sterility, we have to consider two differing images of that shrine to architectural perfection—the Parthenon. Perceived through puritan eyes of the modern architect, it epitomizes a zenith in spatial-formal purity, and functions as a study source in monochromatic excellence. However, through the eyes of its designers, Ictinus and Callicrates, it was completely colour-washed and gilded—its decorative elements detailed in primary hues. They would have been puzzled by its modern perception for, on its opening day in 447 B.C., they had intended its rich and colourful appearance to represent their concept of purity—for its Greek name implies 'virginity'. Through an informed archaeologist's eye, an ancient Greek city would equate to the exuberance and vulgarity commonly associated with the sensory excitation of a fairground. This is because an ancient conception of urban design was that of a total work of art whose spaces breathed texture, colour and form; rich in sensory experience they were created by multi-disciplined designers who envisaged achievements as a synthesis of painting, sculpture and architecture (fig. 18).

In explaining the modern architects' misconception of the Parthenon the Op artist, Victor Vasarely, has pointed to the bifurcation of the roles of the artist and the

18 Alma-Tadema, *Phideas and the Painting of the Frieze of the Parthenon*. This Victorian painting caused uproar amongst purists in 1868 as it depicts the ancient Greek love of primary colours on the exteriors of their buildings. Courtesy Birmingham City Museums and Art Gallery.

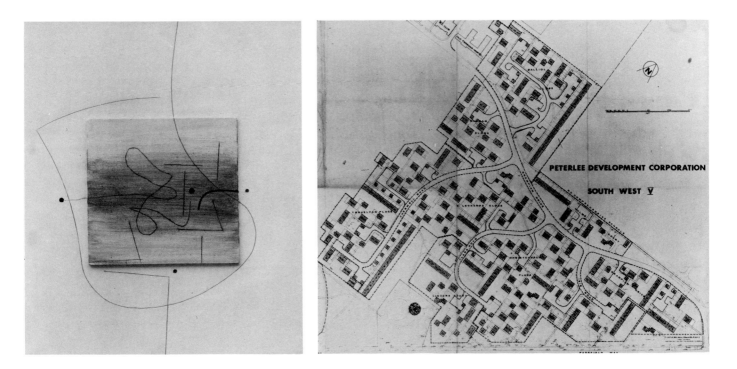

19 One aspect of Victor Pasmore's contributions to the development of Peterlee New Town, County Durham—the close link between elements in his painting and the organization of road systems.
(a) *left* Victor Pasmore, *Linear Symphony*, 1976. Private Collection, USA.
(b) *right* Peterlee Development Corporation South West (phase V). Housing plan designed by Victor Pasmore in co-ordination with Theo Marsden, ARIBA.

architect. He suggests that this separation has its roots in Renaissance Italy, when a new process of making an art-for-its-own-sake was encouraged by a wealthy patronage. Since then, fine art and architecture have pursued separate paths with little interaction—dichotomy depriving the environmental designer of any real expertise in his handling of space. Meanwhile, the sculptor examines the diversity of interplay between solid form, tactile sensation and the empty space surrounding it, while the painter privately investigates colour relationships in the uninhabitable world of two-dimensions. Obviously, the architect can learn much from the artist through, for instance, his incorporation into multi-disciplinary design teams (fig. 19), but he can also gain from a simple study of ordinary people.

For example, in his redefinition of 'defensible space' (as part of an upgrading project for a low-brow housing project in New York City), Oscar Newman discovered amongst his resident-clients a highly favourable response when he intensified their environmental degrees of texture, colour and space. In explaining this response, Newman cites the sociologist, Lee Rainwater, who has projected the ideal of a social ladder of taste in which each rung of society aspires to the one above. According to Rainwater, the architect sits at the top of the ladder and functions as taste-maker, with only the rich and sophisticated having the capacity to enjoy the severity of the concrete existence he tends to disseminate. Meanwhile, the majority at the bottom aspire to the middle-class stratum, and a need for cosiness and variety utilizing colour, texture and appearance is added to their basic drive for shelter. By contrast, Newman claims, bland and anonymous environment is associated in their minds with the austerities of bunkers and prisons.

This basic drive was also encountered in a test monitored by the American colour consultant, Faber Birren, which demonstrated that beneath a superficial layer of good taste—even in the upper class—there lurks a healthy thirst for a decorative diversity in their surroundings. This test centred on the use of two adjacent

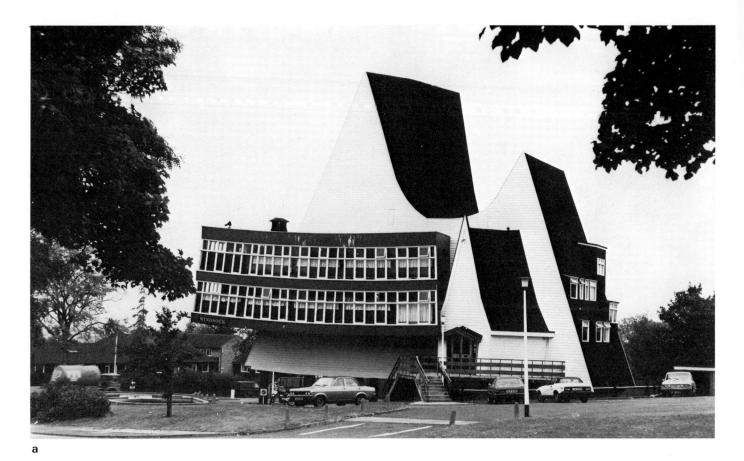

a

20 Diversity in architectural space:
(a) Windsock public house,
Dunstable. Photo: Mike Jenks.
(b) Self-build seaside chalets,
Jaywick Sands. Photo: Mike
Jenks.
Opposite
(c) Fantasy environment, Port
Merion. Photo: Philip Waddy.
(d) Holiday homes, Port Grimaud.
Courtesy Cement & Concrete
Association.

b

54

c

d

55

waiting-rooms; one austere and filled with chrome and leather furniture against white walls, the other 'jazzy' and decorated in heavy colours, chintzy fabrics and kitsch furnishings. During the test, questionnaires and interviews conducted outside the rooms elicited a favourable response to the 'Swedish' style room, but a more discreet surveillance found that the vast majority had actually waited in the 'vulgar' room.

Among the psychological studies which suggest that people have little opportunity for impact on their urban setting, the work of Peter Smith at the University of Sheffield is worth noting. He has made a synoptic study of the primitive or limbic brain —that undernourished portion in the right hemisphere of our grey matter which apparently is deprived of all that sensory stimulation upon which it thrives: richness, ornateness, sparkle and colour. Smith proposes that its poor possessor has, for psycho-physiological stimulation, to escape to spaces in which the volume of its perception is amplified, as it finds little satisfaction in the dull environments created by the brain's dominant and intellectual left hemisphere. He suggests that this escapism partially accounts for the popularity of market-places and the glitter of Piccadilly Circus and Las Vegas. It is also interesting to note that when a group of visitors to Las Vegas (about which we have learned much from Venturi) were interviewed as to why they had come, none of their replies actually mentioned the gambling motive. Instead, they talked of their need for fun and excitement.

Whenever an environment ceases to excite, we find that its inhabitants tend to react both with the aerosol can and, when given the opportunity, with their feet. In order to discover their alternatives we should as designers, observe the kinds of places to which they are attracted. For, in doing so, we discover environments rich in spatial diversity —a glorious, popular architecture of bad taste.

We find this spatial diversification in pleasure environments: fairgrounds, World Fairs, Disney Worlds, Coney Islands and Golden Miles; we can discover them along the American strip where motels and diners take on the forms which remind us of the work of Claes Oldenburg. Along coastlines there is a wealth of a thematic architecture responding to the ocean: ship-shaped *Schooner Inns*, the variegated cabins of Jaywick Sands, Port Grimaud (fig. 20), together with a Scottish boat-shaped castle whose original owner (a seasick Admiral) could survey his fleet from its walls. Meanwhile, inland we can find splendid examples of a Pop architecture: grottoes, follies, and the superb fantasies of Edward James in Mexico and of W. Clough-Ellis in Wales (fig. 20). Most of this alternative architecture compels a response, even if it is only a smile or a raised eyebrow —but some architects are also responding. For example, in describing the Madonna Inn in California, Charles Moore waxed lyrical, 'It is one of the most surprizing (and surprizingly full) experiences to be found.' (fig. 21). The Inn is an extraordinary architecture being designed and built as a labour of love by a family of non-architects. Its interior provides a sumptuous, distinctive fantasy environment. Several of its bedrooms are circular with names like 'Cloud Nine' and 'Vienna Suite'; bathrooms are grotto's with spectacular waterfall toilets and sinks —the Inn being especially renowned for its waterfall urinals (fig. 21).

As part of our education in 'bad taste', let us observe the ways in which people modify their environments in an effort to satisfy the need to personalize and territorialize their homes, especially in monotonous settings. Such a study will find

56

21 (a) *Right* Madonna Inn, San Luis Obispo, California. Courtesy Mr and Mrs Madonna.
(b) *Below* Bathroom grotto, Madonna Inn. Photo: David Brodie.

a

b

22 H.M.S. Verity sculpted in Lonicera, Hanborough, Oxford. Topiary by Arthur Leach who was Leading Seaman on the original vessel. Photo: Iradj Parvaneh.

a wealth of spatial articulation expressed in crazy-paving, fantastic topiary, dream-fulfilling wishing-wells, stick-on Georgian porches and of course, garden gnomes. In taking such loving care in placing these and like objects in space, the ordinary person is a designer being guided, not by profound philosophy, but by a basic, human instinct for a sense of place (fig. 22).

However, to conclude our quest for diversity, here is an example of the total integration of spatial variables in a monument to the non-designer. It stands in a nondescript sector of Los Angeles and was built by an Italian immigrant, Simon Rodia. The towers at Watts have signified many things for many people but, above all, they represent a synthesis between the Renaissance-formed categories of painting (colour), sculpture (surface and form) and architecture (human space) in a single environmental statement (fig. 23). This do-it-yourself structure is also remarkable in that its humble creator constructed it directly into space without the

23 Simon Rodia's Towers at
Watts, Los Angeles; an environmental
fusion of painting, sculpture and
architecture. Photo: Mike Jenks.
Construction details above.

23 Watts Towers: ground level detail.
Photo: Mike Jenks.

Notes
[1] Goldstein, K. 'Some Experimental
Observations Concerning the Influence
of Colour on the Function of the
Organism' *Occupational Therapy and
Rehabilitation*, Volume 21, June, 1942.
[2] Sivik, L. 'Colour Meaning and Perceptual
Colour Dimensions: A Study of Exterior
Colours' *Goteborg Psychology Reports
No. 11*, University of Goteborg, 1974.
[3] Vernon, J. A. *Inside the Black Room*
Clarkson N. Potter, New York, 1963.

aid of scaffolding, machinery or, more interestingly, entirely without any preparatory designs on paper. In speculating on its appearance if Rodia had conceived it via the drawing-board, we would have to study the effects of graphic vehicles on design. It is this consideration that we turn to next.

4   The Spatial Codes

'So-called "modern" architecture has accumulated a formidable reservoir of discontent largely because of its visual austerity.'

Peter Smith, 1974

Whenever the environmental designer is confronted by a design problem his initial solving process involves a visualization of potential solutions. His creative imagination triggers a concept which is imagined ('seen') as a flashing, dimensionless image with the mind's eye —images formed from his creative leap into the proposed environment. These can result from, or be subject to, his prejudices, intuitions, or a systematic analysis or reduction of criteria. Such a mental picture is a photographic impression—incomplete, in a state of flux and somewhat vague; it has originated from many forces at work within his mind including the nature of the immediate problem, his personality traits and past experience —many of these latter influences lying beyond any conscious control. These factors continue to have some bearing on his decision-making throughout the ensuing and evolving sequence of design.

It might be possible to generate and develop images from concepts in the mind alone. But spatial ideas can become so extensive and complex that they can no longer be contained within the mind and have to be externalized. Representation in some tangible form is needed so that they can be clarified, assessed and articulated. At this point the idea has to pass through space and (depending on the designer) be translated into two or three dimensions, as a descriptive model which allows the designer to experience the nature of his idea and develop its conception. This perceived experience, newly-represented, of a form-space acts as the basis for further development inspiring his creative imagination on to other mental images which are, in turn, realized in representational form for personal or group evaluation. This two-way language of design is a continuous dialogue between concept and mode of expression —alternating until the creative process is exhausted.

Through the use of graphics, the architect has traditionally learned to transfer the shifting images of his mind's eye on to the drawing-board. This kind of visualization technique has been commonly accepted as an invaluable design tool and considered as having little effect on the final appearance of architectural form. For example, in addressing students in the 1930s, Le Corbusier explained that architectural form and space is first a concept of the brain, being conceived with the eyes shut; paper was the only means of transmitting spatial ideas back to the designer and to others. If we observe the initial conversion of design concepts into graphic marks we find, more often than not, a use of embryonic ideograms —flow or bubble diagrams and doodled plans. These are simply intended to explore early concepts as patterns of spatial relationships—the cross-section and elevation being introduced as a check on this diagrammatic planning stage.

Depending upon the individual, the conventional design process may also include perspective drawings, isometric or axonometric projections and rough cardboard models which investigate the volumetric implications of a conceived space—but the latter, generally, are only introduced beyond the planning stage.

Representational methods in design seem to supply two types of information: either they describe how a future space might function, i.e., its organizational aspects; or they describe the visual characteristics as perceived by an observer. This chapter examines their application to the conceptual, evaluative and communicative phases of design and also critically assesses their ability to reflect sensations of space.

Conceptual Graphics

The moment an idea is transferred from a designer's mind to an external form is a critical point in the life of any architectural design concept. In order to give birth to the idea he must adopt some form of abstraction which represents or reflects the pictures in his mind. The process of abstraction usually involves a use of descriptive symbols or annotation—images and words which combine to chart the potential relationships between the concept and reality. The diagram appears most useful in these crucial moments for, in functioning as a constructive doodle, it is clearly more concerned with the essence of ideas, than a prediction of appearance.

According to the designer, Keith Albarn, a diagram is evidence of an idea being structured—it is not the idea but a model of it, intended to define its characteristic features. He writes: 'It is a form of communication which increases the pace of development or allows an idea to function and develop for the thinker while offering the possibility of transfer of an idea or triggering of notions.'[1] Albarn concludes by adding: '... through appropriate structuring, it (the diagram) may generate different notions or states of mind in the viewer'. However, these different 'notions or states of mind' are susceptible to three factors which are also rooted in the designer's mind—his familiarity with the mode of expression, the amount of information that it supplies and, embracing all, his previous experience of three-dimensional space.

In order to develop an effective design model and facilitate the evolution of forms in response to this model, a variety of diagrams—each with their own potential and conceptual set of rules which aid decision-making—may be employed:

Schematic or Synthetic Diagrams (fig. 1) are simplified drawings of a concept which stress the relationships and orientation of its physical components. They help the designer to articulate physical forms in response to specific forces such as air and sun movements and views, etc. These types of diagram are usually composed by annotating a schematic drawing with graphic symbols which represent the idea underlying the form. Orthographic or axonometric drawings are frequently employed in this capacity to portray the concrete image; which is then subject to an overlay of the abstract idea.

Project: Imagine an aerial view of a dam. Make a plan of the dam holding back its contents from a dry canyon. The dam suddenly bursts and its waters gush into a rock-filled, dry river bed. Diagram the action of the rushing water as it floods

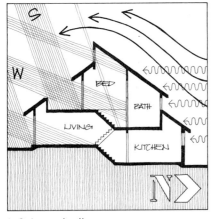

1 Schematic diagram.

2 Operational diagram.

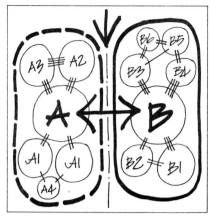

3 Functional diagram.

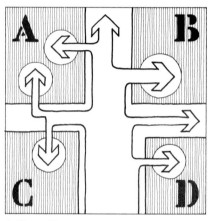

4 Flow diagram.

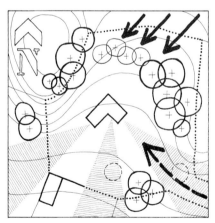

5 Analytical diagram.
Diagram material courtesy William Tilson.

around the rocks and into the canyon. Operational Diagrams (fig. 2) are examples of another conceptual model which aid the designer in visualizing changes in time. They begin to explain the mechanics of a concept, how its elements are manipulated and transformed, and include 'exploded' and 'x-ray' drawings and thumbnail axonometrics and perspectives.

Project: Communicate diagrammatically how to tie a shoelace, or how to replace the blade in a cutting knife, or how to neck-tie a Windsor knot.

Functional Diagrams (fig. 3) identify the proximity and relative size of zones of activity. They are usually called 'bubble-diagrams' and represent the plan in embryo for, as they evolve, the bubbles can metamorphose into finite shapes. These are then dimensioned and given openings—the resultant plan then being vertically extruded and given a lid before being re-examined in other graphic modes. This process is a kind of design sequence in miniature—a route in which the archetypal doodle plays such a major role.

Project: Diagram the anatomy of a small environment such as a country village. This drawing could schematically identify the shape of its inter-related working parts. For example, its spatial mechanism might comprise of a 'nerve-centre' or 'heart' (pub, church, market-place, cross-roads); 'lungs' (village green, playground, park); 'arteries' (footpaths, waterways, road systems); its 'distinguishing marks' (nodal monuments, trees, or steeple), etc.

Flow Diagrams (fig. 4) are, like their 'operational' counterpart, four-dimensional in that they can identify changes over time. They are often used to study direction, intensity, conflicts, problems and possibilities that arise when movement is considered between one point and another, e.g. pedestrian, transport, information, air and water currents, etc. These diagrams can be used in the abstract or superimposed over other drawings when relating information.

Project: Using a flow diagram, track and superimpose a sequence of inter-related movement patterns between major activity centres within a room (bed, radio, wardrobe, chair, window, door). Using further flow diagrams, attempt to economize on the amount of movement by improving the spatial relationship of the objects.

Analytical Diagrams (fig. 5) are useful in visually identifying and relating design constraints which have an influence on an evolving conception. Their salient function lies in the investigation of the nature of existing conditions, such as the proposed site for a building, and to compare and evaluate a completed design with its original intentions.

Project: Standing in the middle of a space which is partially enclosed by trees, make a 'spatial boundary diagram' (similar to the one introduced in Chapter Two). Next, superimpose a second diagram of the same space, but this time base its visual parameters on how you think its relative shape would change in another season, say, without foliage in winter.

Since we can never deal directly with reality at the conceptual stage and must describe and manipulate it through abstract means, any thorough investigation of a concept must, therefore, call on a wide range of descriptive methods. As signs and symbols are merely representations of an idea, obviously in diagramming we must utilize forms which are expressive in relation to the level of abstraction. The ambiguity of these forms can aid conceptualization by offering alternatives or generating new ideas but, when used to communicate ideas to others, can become a liability.

The following exercise is suggested as both a means of developing a personal language of abstract design and of testing its powers of communication. Its origin lies in the design philosophy of the Bauhaus teacher, Johannes Itten, but its value is as relevant now as it was in the 1920s.

Project: Communication of Basic Concepts
Within a series of fifteen frames (either circles or squares) graphically communicate each of the following contrasting concepts: high-low, up-down, flying-falling, vertical-horizontal, over-under, heavy-light, transparent-opaque, fast-slow, order-chaos, rough-smooth, hard-soft, straight-bent, in-out, advancing-receding, sweet-sour.

None of the images should be figurative, i.e., referring to known objects in the real world, nor include words, but should be comprised of pure, abstract symbols which attempt to define clearly the difference between each word-pair and the subtle differences between the fifteen concepts. The similarity between several of

6 Student attempt to communicate six of the antonym concepts using two shapes.

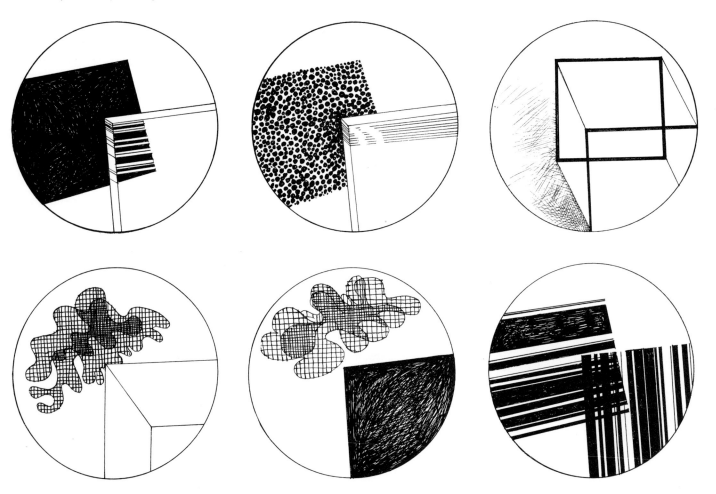

64

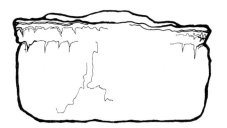

Front Elevation

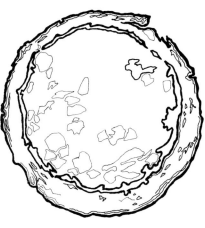

Plan

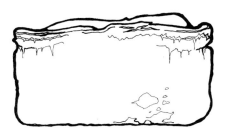

Side Elevation

Section

7 Conventional orthographic display of a meat pie.

the antonyms contained in the list is intentional, its compilation being devised to test your ability to communicate subtle but specific ideas. Some of the diagrams could be worked in black and white but the separation of contrasting concepts could be extended through use of colour. In urging students to incorporate colour in their design process, Le Corbusier once wrote: '. . . with colour you accentuate, you classify, you disentangle. With black you get stuck in the mud and you are lost. Always say to yourself: 'Drawings must be easy to read'. Colour will come to your rescue.'[2] The project should, therefore, utilize a whole range of graphic and mixed-media: paint, ink, chalk, graphite, spray, collage, etc.

On completion of the project, invite a person who has no knowledge of the assignment to match the list of antonyms to your set of diagrams. Only at this stage will your powers of graphic communication within a basic language of design be truly tested! (fig. 6).

Concepts as Orthographics

As the initial scribbles on paper prepare the way for the development of ideas, the next drawing stage sets out concepts more formally. But, as design ideas begin to solidify, so they become less susceptible to any change. The next exercise examines the role of spatial codes used in transferring the concept from its fluid state into the focus of orthographic projection.

Project: The Plan, Section, Elevation and Isometric
For this investigation we need to acquire an object which, in a tangible form, will symbolize a physical model of a design concept. This could be something quite commonplace like a fruit pie, a sandwich or a green pepper. To a lesser or greater degree, each of these objects contains inner cavities which will, for the sake of this exercise, represent the space within a building.

Stage One: draw to full-size (or larger) a plan, together with a cross-section and four elevations, of your selected model. Obviously, your plan will vary in character depending on your choice of object but it should be made at a point just above its base. Your section can be drawn after cutting the object through its middle with a knife, and your elevations made by reconnecting the two halves and viewing from four sides. The drawings should be made in pencil or pen, and at this stage only line intensity should be used to convey depth.

The resulting set of drawings represents the conventions of orthographic projection (fig. 7). It is immediately evident that these spatial codes can only convey physical dimensions because they disregard both your dynamic relationship in terms of distance from and movement around the object and your viewing inclination. The plan, therefore, can only be regarded as a horizontal slice through three-dimensions whilst the section, in conceptually behaving exactly like your cutting knife, is a vertical slice which exposes the guts of mass. The elevations represent external appearance produced on a vertical plane by the projection of parallel sight lines. Within the traditional mode these graphics are, more often than not, drawn in monochrome and in line and retain this diagrammatic quality throughout. However, if we compare our set of drawings with the real object, we find that, quite apart from the obvious absence of such primary cues as binocular and movement parallax, many secondary cues are missing, for example, apparent size given by light and shadow or the inclusion of background information.

65

Similarly, tonal shading would give a linear perspective. Visual characteristics such as surface quality, texture or colour are not accounted for, but these could be included to intensify the images.

Stage Two: working objectively from the actual pie, sandwich or pepper, extend the visual information of the plan, section and elevation through the introduction of colour (coloured pencils, paints, inks, markers) or tone (graphite, conte, charcoal, ink). The transposition of spatial concepts into the dimensions of colour and tone will increase their power of communication in our two-way dialogue of design.

Stage Three: transfer your concept into the multi-dimensions of an axonometric or isometric drawing. This is to help understand the format: often someone asked to imagine and draw a cube visualizes it in isometric form. Similarly, when emergent space is transferred from the fluid conceptual diagram to a three-dimensional graphic schema, the parallel-line framework of the isometric tends to define the concept (fig. 8).

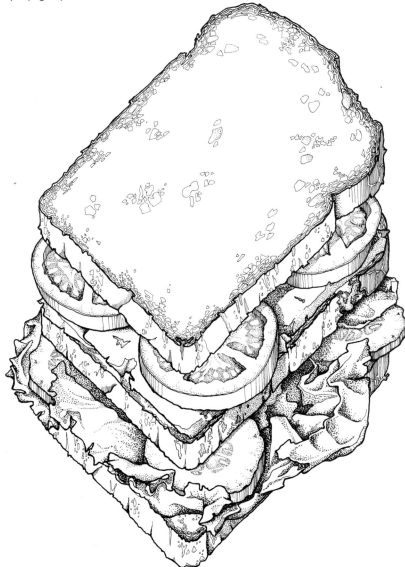

8 Triple-decker sandwich axonometric.

The axonometric and isometric projections are drawings from which the third dimension is inferred —the physical dimensions of length, breadth and height are recorded within one projection. In axonometric drawings the effect of depth is obtained by adding the third dimension —usually to a plan. The plan is set at an angle to the horizontal and heights extruded (fig. 9) from the same axis. In isometric drawings a form would be viewed symmetrically so that all its edges appear to have the same length, i.e., they are all at the same angle to the picture-plane. As its name implies, all planes are drawn to the same length (fig. 9). This ability to represent simultaneously three dimensions enables spaces to be organized in volumetrics rather than in area. But isometrics should not be considered as analogous to visual perception. Isometric viewpoints are monocular, static and fixed. Again, aerial perspective may be represented but linear perspective is ignored —the form-space retaining its size without any concession to foreshortening (although this could be seen as some compensation for constancy scaling). In linear form, these projections appear devoid of all cues to depth apart from that of overlap but they compel powerful sensations of space. However, this compulsion is in our mind's eye and results from its conditioning to the parallelogram or rhombus as a rectangle seen as occupying space —for even when all depth cues are absent, the parallelogram continues to retain spatial meaning.

Some difficulty might have been experienced in transposing the source object into the isometric format. This is because isometrics are not usually used as representations of existing objects, being more exclusively employed as vehicles for ideas (fig. 10). The distortion encountered in transferring objective information makes an interesting comparison with the transfer of concepts because the latter, being in a fluid state, is possibly least resistant to its configuration. If, for the exercise, you had chosen a circular sandwich or pie or, indeed, the green pepper, you might have experienced an even greater difficulty in drawing the three-dimensional form within the rigidity of the isometric. Possibly, you will have had to suspend the impression within the linear framework of a transparent box; this rectilinear overlay on a curvilinear form can straightjacket any non-conformist idea in embryo, for when later removing the box construction lines (thus removing the parallelograms) you risked divesting the isometric of its spatial meaning and increasing its distortion.

Stage Four: eat the object of the exercise!

After disposing of the model we are left, apart from our memory, with a summary in orthographics of its existence. The set of drawings remain as evidence of our previous sensory experience and equate to the level of information we can expect in a design process. In order to re-experience a concept presented in orthographics we have to translate the drawings by mentally co-ordinating the plan with the section and elevations, the isometric providing a single, distorted glimpse of its third dimension.

This mental co-ordination of single-view drawings can induce a fragmented approach to spatial organization. For example, it can lead to separate level design in planning space; an attitude in which a concept is considered as a number of layers —a stack of sandwiches —each conceived independently, with the elevations functioning as wrapping-paper to bind them together, so that elevations are seen as individual planes, unrelated to other surfaces and disconnected from interior space. But our built environment is most at risk from a further side-effect,

9 Two concept containers offering slightly different visualizations of an idea.

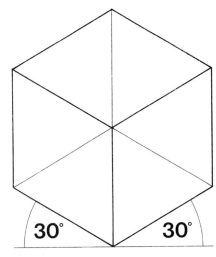

Isometric

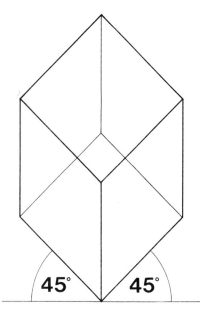

Axonometric

10 A design concept encased in an isometric container. Laszlo Moholy-Nagy, *Light requirement for an Electric Stage*, 1922–30. Courtesy Bauhaus Archiv.

11 The two elevations used in Victor Papanek's test—and the two possible solutions.

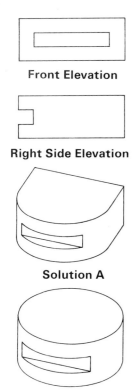

Front Elevation

Right Side Elevation

Solution A

Solution B

that of squareness, an effect that relates to our apparent inability to visualize forms which exist beyond the influence of the right-angle. This was demonstrated by Victor Papanek who, in his book *Design for the Real World*, described an experiment in which students were asked to interpret the information provided by a front and side elevation (fig. 11a). Due to its ambiguity two solutions are possible (fig. 11b) and Papanek found that more architects and draughtsmen failed to arrive at the more 'elegant' solution (the lower version) than those uninitiated into orthographics. Because of the lack of depth cues in the elevations, the designer subjects had assumed that they described a squareness or rectangularity —being unable to visualize alternative forms.

The elevations used in Papanek's test belong to the ambiguous language of spatial codes —a language which makes it difficult for its user to conceive of space other than that complementary to its descriptive powers. At its worst, the Modern Movement's infatuation with a simplistic philosophy has often resulted in the monotonous but orthographic projection may be as much to blame. At best, we can find examples of its effect in the work of more creative designers. For example, Walter Gropius, in designing the interior of the Director's Office in the Weimar Bauhaus, expressed a design philosophy which appears inextricably knitted into the mechanics of an isometric. The horizontal planes in Frank Lloyd Wright's designs seems to derive their pleasure from elevation drawing, and the sawn-off appearance of several of Paul Rudolph's buildings enjoy exposing their inner cells in the manner of the cross-section. According to Charles Jenks, 'Stirling's work is rooted in his techniques of drafting: the method leads to the

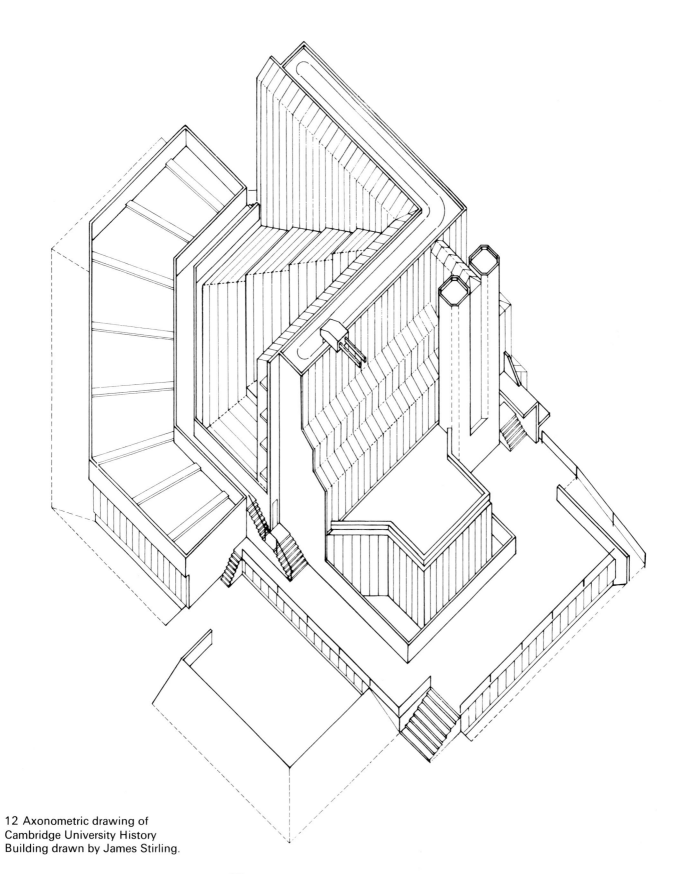

12 Axonometric drawing of
Cambridge University History
Building drawn by James Stirling.

15 *Opposite:* Coke can study: a page from an exhaustive student sketchbook exercise.

form.' Jim Stirling's love of minimal, dead-pan axonometrics speaks for itself—the edges of his buildings closely following the angles and axes of their former representations (fig. 12). Meanwhile, a post-Modernist approach pushes the descriptive potential of orthographics to their limits; their plans, sections, elevations and axonometrics tend to be loaded with depth information — and conceived in colour. One facet of a new quest for environmental diversity is a more polychromatic architecture. However, the potential of any three-dimensional idea in flux requires a more dynamic articulation than the single, static view used by many designers.

Dynamic Graphics: Concepts in Motion

If we want to appreciate a concept fully we need to experience it from all sides and at all angles, turning the object in our mind before its transfer and subsequent articulation in graphics. For the purpose of an animated perception, varieties of isometrics and, indeed, perspectives are employed—their frames of reference or vanishing points being mobilized through sequential drawings which assess the implications of an idea in the round.

The next project includes a short series of exercises which are simply intended as mental gymnastics:

Project: Movement in Subjective and Objective Space

(a) Imagine a three-dimensional object capable of penetrating a square, circular, and triangular shaped hole—each of equal area. In passing through, its form should exactly fit each of the differing apertures—the correct form obviously having to comprise of elevations drawn from the shapes of the three holes. (For the solution refer to fig. 13 on page 73.)

(b) Imagine a rotating cube invisibly suspended from one of its corners; compare the experience of movement, as alternation, when viewing the Necker Cube (fig. 14). Make a series of silhouette drawings which, in shape, describe in sequence a single revolution (if your visualization breaks down, make a small cube model for reference and complete the sequence).

(c) Get to know an object. Using an ink bottle, a paint tube, a shoe, a piece of stone, a bent Coke can or any everyday object, make a series of objective pencil drawings from all angles which attempt to communicate its totality (fig. 15).

(d) Design a comic-strip scenario for an imaginary animated film using a set of abstract components as a starting point. An excellent choice for the first frame is a Constructivist painting, for example, one of twenty 'stills', the possibilities of interelated movements in which various components spiral, fly and weave trajectories plotted within the space of each frame. Some forms could travel towards the observer, filling the frame and then moving on; others could zoom into the distance while still others journey across the frame —each animated unit finally coming to rest in the positions assumed in the first frame (fig. 16). (El Lissitzky would have thoroughly approved this animation of his work as he was fascinated by the kinetic potential of basic forms—giving his graphic work narrative titles such as 'The Adventures of a Square'.)

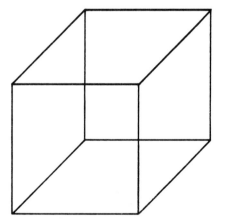

14 The common method of graphically describing a cube is, paradoxically, the ambiguous Necker cube with alternating faces.

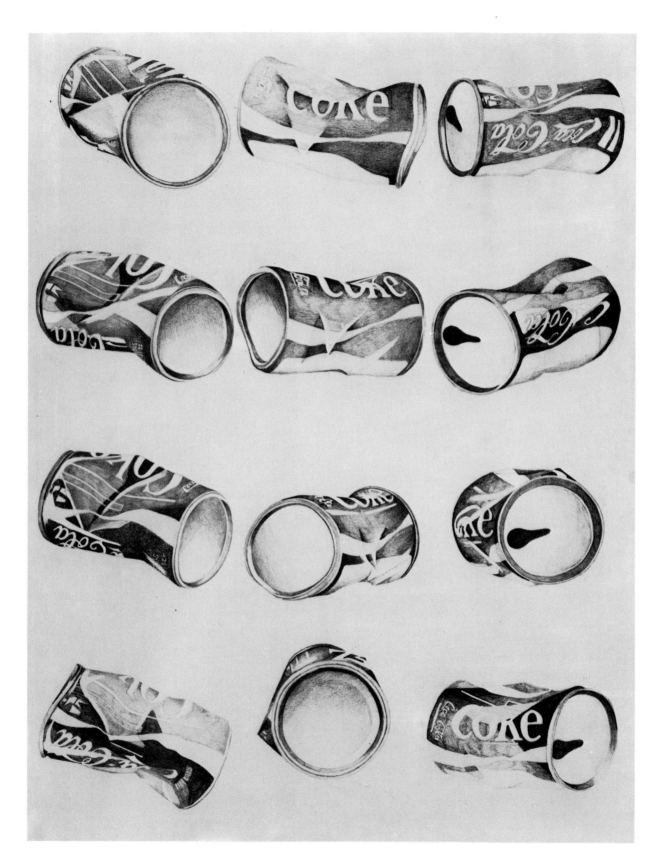

71

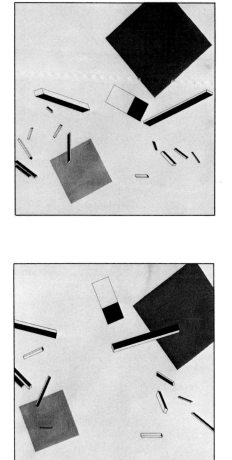

16 Three 'stills' from a student project animating El Lissitzky's *Of Two Squares*, 1920.

In a documentary film on his life and work, the sculptor, Henry Moore acknowledged the range of drawings required to account adequately for more intricate forms. He described his need to create for a single sculpture up to forty, fifty, or even hundreds of drawings to convey its complexity. He was, for instance, motivated by the interplay of space and form generated by an elephant's skull. The designer, Keith Albarn has also suggested the importance of investigating ideas more fully and in a range of sizes, and devised a basic design teaching method for the all-round analysis of a cuboid concept. He describes a backing sheet containing different orthographic views of a cube shape: at top-left a square (the one face elevation), at top-right and bottom-left a rectangle divided by a line (two double-face elevations), and at bottom-right a hexagon with three divisions (isometric view). Design ideas can be worked on an overlay sheet and related to the four views (fig. 17). He suggests that this simple, four-stage 'turning' process of architectureal ideas is a two-dimensional representation of a three-dimensional representation of a four-dimensional reality.

Historical attempts at recording movement on the two-dimensional plane include the multi-legged, running bison of prehistoric cave painting; the 'echo' lines of animated objects in strip cartoons; the nude who, in the time-exposure of Marcel Duchamp's perception, descended a painted staircase; and the optical

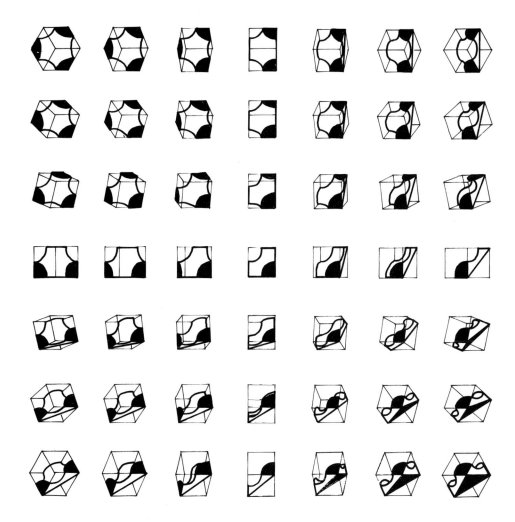

17 A design concept tested 'four-dimensionally' in an extensive range of isometric views; student sculpture project. Courtesy Keith Albarn.

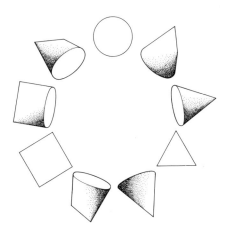

13 The form capable of passing through a square, circular and triangular aperture.

shifts and jumps of visual disturbance created by the Op artists. Central to this development in modern art was the Cubist style, acclaimed as a new vision that redefined perceptual form in painting and created a new language of liberated expression that could make a composite image of a total experience. In its Analytical phase, the appearance of an object in actual space was directly transposed piece by piece into pictorial space. However, once Cubism became dissociated from its strictly representational purpose, it began to flounder. As the movement reached its Synthetic phase, its attention was diverted towards a subjective identity and, despite the efforts of Picasso, its later content seemed naive and unconvincing when compared with contemporary developments in the theatre and, especially, in film.

Although every design student is (or should be) encouraged to own and use a camera, its mechanical images, like drawings, tend to reinforce a fixed, static conception of space by recording only one of the infinite number of views of an object. It is, therefore, even more important to use a movie camera for this will help instill a more profound appreciation of a four-dimensional space. Being unable to photograph our mental concepts, the perspective drawing, especially in the early stages of design, acts as a conceptual camera, used directly to give substance to a new idea or as visual monitor of ideas born of orthographics.

73

Ideas in Perspective

There are many books which deal with perspective. The majority describe its underlying principles through a presentation of its linear projections. This will not be the case here for we move directly to a project which is more concerned with a development of a personal perspective based on direct perception rather than filtered through its mechanical framework.

Project: Sixty, Three-Minute Perspectives

As a prelude to this project, select a route through an urban space, including movement both through the space between and, if possible, inside buildings. Your route might include a variety of architectural experience: spaces between architecture (urban thoroughfares, streets, alleys); thresholds or transitional space (entrances, arcades, cloisters); spaces inside architecture (rooms, corridors, concourses) and, possibly, passing through the suburban edge into parkland, rural landscape or waterfronts.

The main aim of this exercise is to produce a minimum of sixty sketchbook drawings in a variety of media (pen, pencil, charcoal, brush, markers) and sizes during the course of your journey, each drawing taking no more than three minutes in its execution!

Make the first drawing at your pre-selected starting-point and viewing the first section of your proposed route. Working quickly, attempt to record the essential ingredients of the space. There is no time to spend on irrelevant details. After three minutes have elapsed (signalling the end of a drawing) move on into the space and make a second from inside the view already recorded so that this drawing picks up the spatial continuum of the last —and so on. In other words, each subsequent drawing describes a new spatial sensation —either as an extension or a change of direction from that of its predecessor. The speed of the drawing is central to the study and necessary in short-circuiting any inhibitions associated with perspective; their rapidity forces a personal process of selection, i.e., the visual extraction and graphic transmission of essential information from perception to drawing.

The first thirty drawings could be made purely in line, some concentrating on horizontal or vertical dynamics of the view (fig. 18), others describing architectural

19 John Bratby, *Window, Self-Portrait, Jean and Hands,* 1957. Oil on board, 48 × 144 in. Courtesy The Tate Gallery.

74

18 Three-minute drawings exploring
horizontal dynamics, vertical mass
and light and shade: student
project.

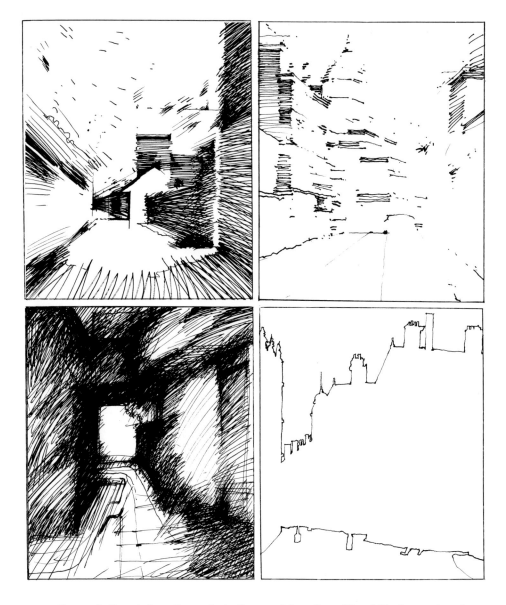

mass through the delineation of skyline and baseline (fig. 18). Later drawings
could translate light and shadow patterns in tone while others record space in
colour. In the final stage, your angle of vision could deviate to include close-ups,
such as architectural details or floorscape patterns. Your set of sixty drawings could
also include experiments with the extent of your visual field contained within the
frame. For example, the painter John Bratby made a series of drawings and
paintings whose frames encompassed, not only the subject matter at or near his
centre of vision, but a detailed account of what lay around its edge —his own feet,
legs, and even the drawing on which his hand worked! (fig. 19). In this manner,
one can question a tradition which has dictated what should, and what should not,
be contained within the limits of a pictorial image.

On completing this project, compare the early drawings with those worked
towards its finale. There should be increasing evidence of conviction in their
execution together with a corresponding completeness of visual information

75

20 *Nude in the Garden*. Roger C. Ferri's perspective of a courtyard—one of six groves surrounding his design for a museum complex, Los Angeles.

collected en route. It is with the support of such an experience that we can now argue the pro's and con's of perspective projection.

The convention of perspective projection is based upon the way in which the human eye perceives parallel lines as converging with distance. This representation of linear perspective, as a constant relationship between apparent size and distance, is normally constructed showing horizontal lines subject to convergence whilst vertical lines remain constant. Perspectives are generally associated with visual experience as opposed to the physical organization of designed space. Although lacking primary cues to depth, they can lend themselves to more pictorial illustration (shading, texture, colour) and utilization of the secondary cues than other drawings (figs 20). However, when compared with visual perception, perspectives do not accommodate for constancy scaling for —like a photograph — they only represent the retinal image on the eye and not the brains' compensatory modification for distance. Thus a perspective is strictly valid for a single eye —fixed by its monocular co-ordinates.

A perspective drawing provides a small conical or pyramidal view within our

76

20 Perspective of living room,
Boudov Residence, Palos Verdes,
California, 1976. Designed by Coy
Howard; drawing by Coy Howard
and Sherwood Roper.

hemisphere of vision although the size of a drawing and the assumed proximity of
an observer can both affect the degree of simulation. When using them in sketch
form, design ideas can be influenced by a need to compose pleasing images on
paper—thus contorting a concept and misleading the designer. This graphic form of
misrepresentation includes the infamous artist's impression which can convey a
dreamworld distortion to both the unwitting designer and an innocent public.
Graphic seduction extends far beyond the colourful impressions of holiday hotels
(even if unbuilt or incomplete) of the glossy travel brochure, and the contrived
perspectives of desirable property column dwellings—it can exist on the
architect's drawing-board where the artist himself is deceived.

Accurate perspectives are often easier to construct from positions from which, in
reality, a space would never be viewed. This is particularly true of interiors where the
vantage points are either located outside the space with one wall removed or, if
inside, with the observer impossibly built into the wall. So there is an evident
danger of the designer being encouraged, not only to visualize his spaces from
exterior points, but also to fashion his ideas from unlikely stances. And, as the laws of

convergence in linear perspective are commonly applied to only horizontal lines, he may disregard vertical convergence. Parallel verticals appear as correct in perspectives of low buildings but when applied to tall buildings they appear rather strange. In consequence, it might be argued, architects adept at stylized perspectives which ignore vertical convergence have a predilection for a squat, horizontal architecture.

Apart from the use of perspective drawings in communicating resolved design ideas, possibly their greatest asset is their speed and ease of production in sketch form at conceptual stages. They are often of use to the designer who needs rapid visual feedback. The need to develop a personal approach in their use, therefore, is important because many such drawings fail to show more than the skeletal starkness of technical drawing. However, at whatever stage of use, their powers of spatial communication, as with all graphics, are positively linked to their translation capacity — both of the mind's eye of their creator and that of any subsequent beholder!

In comparing the communication prowess of drawings and models, an Oxford experiment by F. Batterton and K. Whiting produced some interesting results. Groups of designer subjects were first set the task of translating (without representational aids) ten verbally instructed stages in the dissection of a cube. Each stage described an increasingly more complex cut, necessitating the mental retention and continued turning of the impression in the mind's eye. At the stage when unaided visualization broke down, subjects were given a pencil and paper and, again, when this was found inadequate, they were handed a block of plasticine and a knife. A second test examined the comparative strike-rate between unaided, graphic and model sequences.

The findings demonstrated that both graphical and physical models had outstripped the progress of unaided visualization. However, in all cases, use of a three-dimensional model enabled subjects to complete the entire sequence quickly and correctly. Batterton and Whiting speculate that, if graphic techniques are the sole method employed in design, alternative solutions which might exist beyond their capacity could remain hidden or even ignored. This supposition is echoed by the documented observations of many design tutors who find that their students tend to be more spontaneously diverse in their ideas and accelerated in their development when working in three dimensions.

Graphic modes of spatial representation can break down when faced with complex forms —a redundancy point at which creative designers turn to other media. For example, Louis Kahn, himself an influential draughtsman, encountered the futility of perspective views whilst attempting to describe a complicated structure of tetrahedrons and turned, instead, to the medium of models. Within the work of some contemporary designers such as Denys Lasdun and Norman Foster, models play a central role in conceptual and generative design development. In other fields where spatial conflict is critical —as in aeroplane, ship, car, furniture and industrial design —models are well-established design tools but in architecture they are not in widespread use —especially to witness the birth of an idea.

Concepts in the Third Dimension (Scale Models)
Depending upon their stage of use and application within a design process, architectural models fall into various types. For instance, conceptual models (fig.

23 1:20 skeletal model of the structure and cladding for the Sainsbury Centre for Visual Arts, University of East Anglia, Foster Associates. Photo: John Donat.

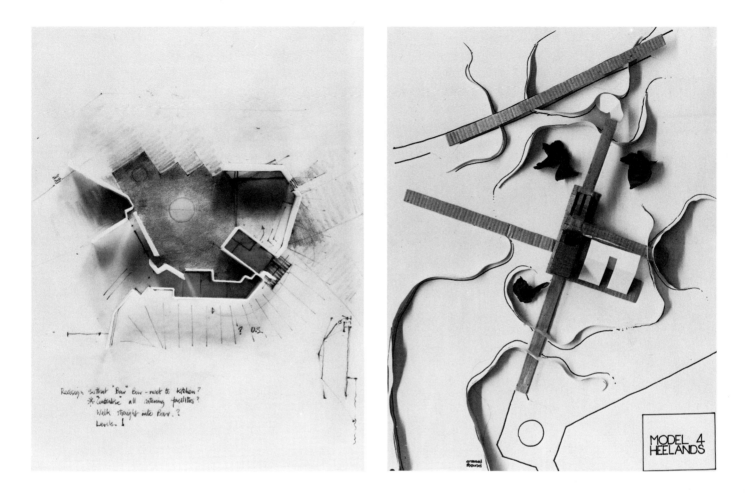

MODEL 4
HEELANDS

21) are three-dimensional diagrams fabricated when an idea is still fragile. In its basic form, it can be seen in operation at the dining-table when, in earnest conversation, people spontaneously use condiments and cutlery to illustrate a topographical point under discussion. Similarly, in design, physical diagrams are usually constructed quickly with junk or mixed-media to symbolize the components and relationships of an idea. On the other hand, block models (fig. 22) carve the external mass of an idea and can include a study of its implications in relation both to the site-space and to that of surrounding mass. By contrast, skeletal models (fig. 23) examine functional determinants in isolation from surrounding features. They can act as three-dimensional bubble-diagrams in studying activity zones; or physical working-drawings in studying structure, assembly, or service systems. The space model (fig. 24) articulates the interaction of plane and surface in both interior and exterior, individual or sequential space. More sophisticated versions are employed in simulating natural and artificial lighting conditions. Presentation models (fig. 25) represent the total composition of an architectural solution and communicate its finality to others. They take the form of miniature prefigurations of an architecture represented in detail and as a complete entity. Being primarily built for promotion rather than decision-making they are less flexible than the rest and are usually intended to convey qualities of external form and its relationships. More complicated knockdown versions can

21 *Above left*
Conceptual model functioning as a three-dimensional diagram—from the initial phase of a design project in which a student has simply developed a sketch into a small model. Photo: Iradj Parvaneh.

22 *Above right*
Block model projecting an evolving design idea: student project. Photo: Iradj Parvaneh.

24 Space model of display panels used as a design tool in the interior design of the Sainsbury Centre. A full-size mock-up of the panels can be seen in the lower gallery. Courtesy Foster Associates.

25 Presentation model. National Theatre and Opera House on an originally proposed London site viewed from Westminster Bridge, 1965. Denys Lasdun & Partners. Photo: Robert Kirkman.

also be presented so that a closer examination of their internal workings can be achieved.

Project: Tree House (Space Model)
Materials: strips of softwood (possibly from an old crate), bamboo, balsa wood, plastic straws, string, wire, and some pieces of canvas or nylon, also a cutting knife, a small saw, and a stout base-board.

Stage One: a tree house would require a tree, therefore, for this project we need to obtain a branch which, like its smaller component—the leaf, is a representational element of its parent form but in a diminished configuration. The branch could be up to four feet tall and culled from a mature or, preferably, a dead tree; its selective pruning being governed by the very nature of the assignment. The branch should then be 'planted' at the centre of the base-board and grafted by wiring, screwing or nailing from below. Next, consider the space contained within and generated around the tree form. For example, if we examine our hand grasping an imaginary ball, the concept of roundness can be identified in the character of the contained space defined by fingers and palm. Similarly, within the geometry of the tree's limbs we find contained an interelated continuum of positive space pockets which, when conceptually enlarged to human scale, function as the design potential for the tree house. In order to maintain a fix on this enlarged sense of scale, make a representative cut-out cardboard figure which can act as a check against your development of its space.

Stage Two: without the aid of any preliminary sketches or drawings, begin to pursue initial ideas for a single-cell house which, in working directly into the model of the tree, allows an unrestricted dialogue between concepts, materials, and the potential of the host support. For instance, the house need not have walls or roof· but might utilize either a natural foliage or a demountable canvas canopy—its functional space being designed on the idea of providing an elevated rest or play platform for two or three children or adults. Through a process of trial and error, planar relationships could be evolved which extend the spatial geometry of the tree as opposed to the insensitive planting of a built form which might work equally well on the ground. Connections and jointing both between building materials and their supporting members should employ sympathetic techniques such as lashing which, in reality, would respect the tree and allow it and its new offspring to kinesthetically co-exist (fig. 26).

By working directly in space, concepts are formed and re-shaped as a result of their immersion in three-dimensions; a process in which options remain open in design routes—options which might not appear available to the designer trapped within the confines of paper. A similar spatial approach is reflected in primitive, especially nomadic architecture, and is also central to the sprouting of hand-made houses and in the heavily publicized art of the architectural wood butcher.

However, it would be interesting to test again the orthographic codes by translating your tree house design back into the world of two-dimensions. And, through the plan, section, and elevation, make an attempt to recommunicate the design graphically. If, by any chance, such graphic displays appear unable to cope with the diversity of your form, make a sequence of sketchbook perspectives which—from a range of vantage points (including its view from below)—establish its changing impression. It is this constant movement between a two and

26 Two tree houses: student project.
Photo's: Iradj Parvaneh.

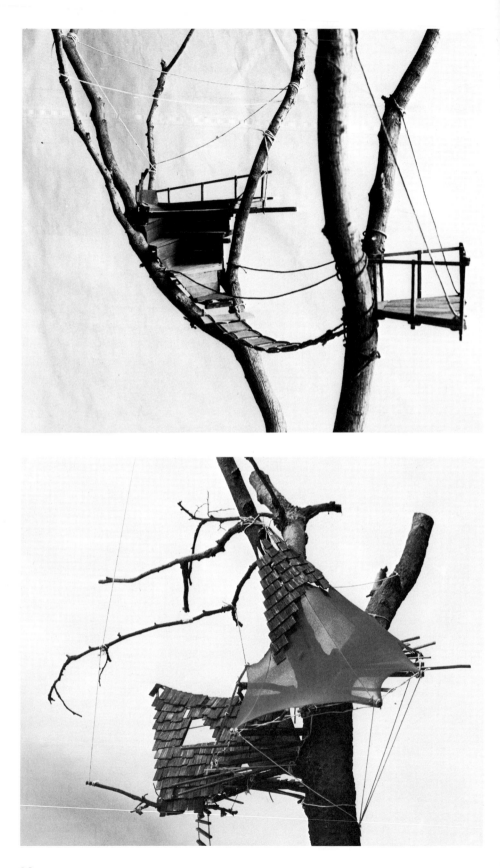

three-dimensional interpretation of design ideas which both intensifies and informs the quality of subsequent experience.

Quite apart from providing a cross-checking facility between physical and visual information, models allow visual and physical movement around projected buildings and, via viewing devices, close scrutiny of and movement within interiors. The primary depth cue of binocular parallax exists in models together with linear perspective, overlap and, light and shade. However, the principal difference between a model (and, indeed, a drawing) and its anticipated final form is one of scale. For, with a diminuitive scale, binocular parallax misrepresents through too much vision. For example, if we look at a pencil, due to its size in relation to the distance between our eyes, it is possible to see slightly more than half-way around its stem: now imagine that the pencil represents a building component, say a column in model form. So we can understand that when viewing a complete model of a building, our field of vision can include a far greater amount of spatial information than when viewing an actual building. The scrutiny of models with our naked eyes, therefore, can induce binocular distortion —the interocular distance between our eyes emphasizing the difference in scale.

Rich displays of spatial intricacy can side-track the designer into a fascination with 'miniaturism' —an attitude associated with the discrepancy between human and model scales. This effect puts the designer outside his concept by interposing a distance known as the 'Gulliver Gap'. Artists are fully aware of the fact that the significance of an idea in cartoon or maquette form may be lost or reduced when enlarged to full-size; as the scale of a painting, a sculpture, and a building is increased, so the amount of information within the field of vision reduces proportionally —often relegating a seemingly exciting idea to the mundane. As a means of compensation, many architects make models large enough to accept the head and so simulate interior eye level views; others have been known to attempt a bridging of the gap by peering at model exteriors down the wrong end of binoculars. But the most useful device for surmounting the scale barrier is the modelscope, which transports the mind's eye directly into a model space. Modelscopes are miniature periscopes which, when inserted into models, provide selective and realistic images. Movement through model-space can also be simulated by the simple operation of panning and tracking. These views can be photographed by attaching a camera but the resulting circular photographs tend to be of rather poor quality with distortion occurring around the edge. A modelscope designer, Richard A. Abbott, suggests that improved photographs can be accomplished by the production of composite pictures, i.e., panoramic views built-up of successive exposures providing one hundred degrees of vision (fig. 27).

Obviously, the materials used in model-making will be different from those in reality but they provide the designer with the tactile experience of shaping physical space. Nevertheless, a model-making fabric can influence the quality of the architecture it replicates. For instance, critics have blamed the proliferation of a severe, Brutalist architecture on the widespread use of balsa wood for modelling and Oscar Newman, when writing in *Colour for Architecture*, censured those weaned on a Bauhaus tradition who, relying on grey, cardboard models, spread the anonymity of a raw, concrete environment. Effects of model-making materials have been noted by the industrial designer, John Gaylard, in the context of international car design. He suggests that the considerable skill in plaster modelling developed

by Italian designers has produced cars with sharp, crisp edges; whilst the Americans, who usually use 'American Wax', created designs with softer, more rounded edges. British designers, on the other hand, have traditionally employed timber prototypes which achieve a finish reflecting something of a compromise between the two.

Any comparison between models and drawings shows that both have advantages. Models incorporate spatial information in a form more easily interpreted, especially by laymen, and embody the third dimension denied to graphics. However, the portability and reproducability of drawings, together with their ease of updating (it being quicker to change a line than rebuild a model) probably accounts for their prevalence in architectural design. Often they are used in interaction, as in plane design where literally tens of thousands of orthographic drawings are produced in conjunction with models of all scales—from wind-tunnel prototypes to full-size mock-ups. In television scenery design, plans and elevations of sets are cut out, glued on card, then assembled into scale versions of productions so that the choreography (of both cameras and players) can be resolved prior to full-scale construction. The interaction of drawings, models and photography in environmental decision-making can provide a more realistic evaluation. For example, a composite image can be achieved by a superimposing of a drawn design on an actual site photograph, or a photomontage can combine a photograph of a design model with that of its intended site (fig. 28). Alternatively, photographs of site views can be strategically located around the openings of models for an interior photograph (either normal, via the modelscope, or even stereoscopic) to fuse proposed with real impressions. Urban site models could be constructed from photographed, cut-out elevations of existing buildings; the proposed model building being introduced and re-photographed against the real setting. Otherwise, models can be taken to their sites or, at least, photographed out-of-doors against suitable backgrounds such as foliage. An unusual but successful montage was created by one architect to communicate his orthographic drawings of a new aquarium building; he simply superimposed photographs of the drawings over a ciné film he had made of tropical fish swimming around their tank.

84

28 (a) Student photomontage of a design model for a tourist Information Centre located in Carfax, Oxford. Photo: Gordon Shaw.

85

28 (b) Composite perspective looking South from the Summit Garden on Roger C. Ferri's design for a High Rise Tower proposed for Madison Square, New York, N.Y.

(c) City Edges. Civic Sign Project for Philadelphia, 1974. Denese Scott Brown, Paul Hirshorn and Steven Izenour. Courtesy Venturi and Rauch.

This process, at least, recognized the existence of some of his buildings' future occupants.

In announcing the prizewinners in a recent photographic competition for young architects, the judge expressed his shock at discovering so few entrants had submitted photographs which included people. He was astonished that those who purport to design habitation for human beings were so reluctant to recognize their existence in their architectural images. However, quite apart from humanitarian aspects, photographs and drawings perceptually have no inherent scale—it is implied by the observer through reference to familiar objects of known size contained within their pictorial displays. It is wise, therefore to include figures, especially in drawn space, as a check on scale relationships; relationships which, if misconstrued by the designer, can easily be transferred to the built environment. A graphic transfer of concepts should borrow as many secondary cues to depth as possible as a means of enhancing spatial meaning—especially in the formative stages. Throughout the design process graphics can vary according to their function. For instance, at the presentation stage, drawn images might address the

(d) Photomontage of a proposed design for the Science Library Towers, Cambridge, in context with the site seen from Kings College meadows, 1961. Denys Lasdun & Partners. Photo: Arnold Behr.

87

29 (a) Two design schemes for
the renovation of the Lutèce
Restaurant, New York, N.Y. Roger
C. Ferri's drawings were intended
for presentation first to the client—
a chef who does not understand
technical drafting—and then for
the architectural community at
large.

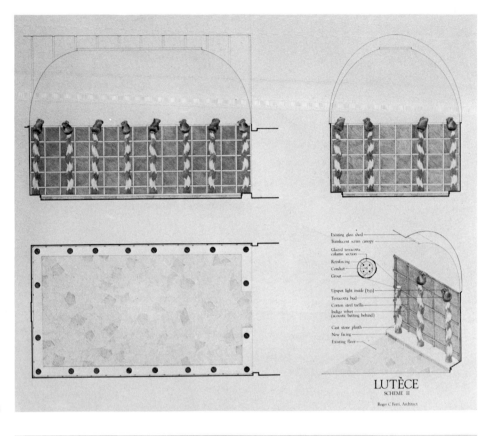

a

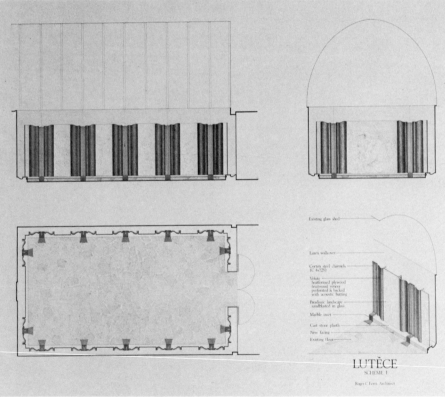

Opposite
(b) Presentation drawings for a
competition. Peter Wilson's plan
and elevations submitted to the
Millbank Competition, London,
1977. Collection The Tehran
Museum of Contemporary Art.

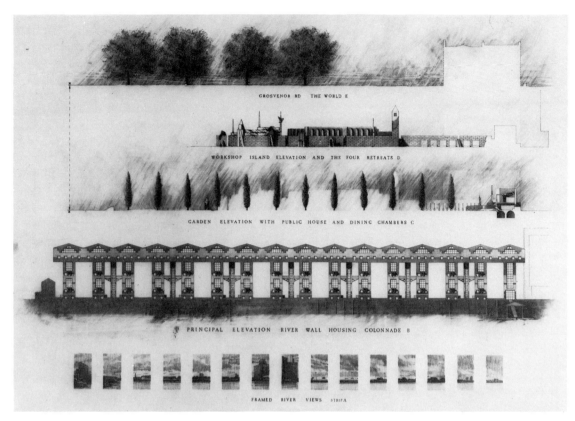

GROSVENOR RD   THE WORLD E

WORKSHOP   ISLAND   ELEVATION   AND   THE   FOUR   RETREATS D

GARDEN   ELEVATION   WITH   PUBLIC   HOUSE   AND   DINING   CHAMBERS C

PRINCIPAL   ELEVATION   RIVER   WALL   HOUSING   COLONNADE B

FRAMED   RIVER   VIEWS   STRIP A

b

problem of 'fit' between mode of visualization, type of problem and the anticipated audience (fig. 29). Colour should also be incorporated into two and three-dimensional representations; its scale can be reduced, particularly in models, along its dimensions of hue, saturation (chroma), brightness (value) using the Munsell notation which charts colour variants.

During more fluid design phases, attempts should be made to appreciate fully the nature of any idea which appears to satisfy initial criteria. For a deeper investigation of its potential the mental kicking around process can be more informed through a subjection to varieties of expressional modes and varieties of size and scale. It is through the adoption of multi-views of its impression and its metamorphic testing along two, three and four dimensions that we allow a new conception to 'breathe' and simultaneously extend our powers of visualization. By making drawings from physical models and transferring graphic information into three-dimensional constructs we also increase our knowledge and experience of media which not only avoids the familiar stylism trap but, within a more creative and developing design dialogue, begins to harness an awareness of appropriate design vehicles to each individual and unique concept of architecture.

It is against this background need to appropriate more suitable examination methods of architectural concepts that recent research into spatial representation is motivated. Various experimental programmes are seeking new ways of revealing embryonic solutions in a format which is aligned both to the nature of the problem and to our perception of reality. It is to this work and its intention of providing the designer with an opportunity of taking a walk around his drawing-board that the concluding chapter is dedicated.

Notes
[1] Albarn, K. and Miall-Smith, J. Diagram: The Instrument of Thought Thames & Hudson, London, 1977.
[2] Le Corbusier For Students Only: If I Had to Teach Students Faber, London, 1954.

5   Simulating 'Real' Space

'Architecture is the ultimate erotic act. Carry it to excess and it will reveal both the traces of reason and the sensual experience of space. Simultaneously.'

Bernard Tschumi, 1976

Much research into spatial representation is based on the premise that designers have long lacked a means for the objective exploration and prediction of the effects of architectural space. Even Le Corbusier admitted to the many surprises which he had encountered after the completion of his buildings—visual anomalies which had not been anticipated nor accounted for within his design sequence. In an increasingly complex and changing environment, contemporary designers are faced, on the one hand, with more complex varieties of existing problems requiring yet more rapid solutions and, on the other, with problems which have yet no basis in previous experience for their solution. This chapter, therefore, describes the ongoing work and research in the development of new ways of overcoming the perceptual limitations of traditional representations by drawings and models. Although all of the methods discussed do not supply a total simulation of our visual, let alone sensory, perception of the real world they do have one aspect of experience in common—that of movement. It is this ability to simulate motion which is vital for at the essence of our understanding of space is our movement within it.

Although the eye is traditionally compared with a camera lens there is an enormous difference between the two. For instance, our eyes are capable of perceiving movement in terms of clearly defined images without the aid of a shutter! The research of Gunnar Johansson of the University of Uppsala, Sweden, has concentrated on this remarkable optical operation in which the eye effortlessly decodes the blur of light streaks entering the retina into a structured perception of space and form. He believes that from an evolutionary standpoint this ability was a necessary part of our biological survival kit for, even in many lower animals, the perception of movement is of decisive importance. Johansson also suggests that a similar dependence on changes in visual stimulus can be demonstrated in man and cites as evidence experiments in which an image held motionless on the retina mechanically seems to fade and disappear. Conversely, our ability to determine visually the precise spatial position of fast moving objects testifies to the fact that the eye is basically an instrument for analysing changes in light flux over time rather than an instrument for recording static images. Although visual information interacts with signals from other sense organs, other experiments have shown that the visual perception of motion is able to override conflicting spatial information from those of other channels.

In the light of the statement by the psychologist, J. J. Gibson, that a motion

91

picture is 'much richer in information than a still picture'[1], the idea of attaching a movie camera to a modelscope as a means of transporting the eye on an animated exploration of the spaces inside and outside scale models becomes an exciting prospect. The possibility of being able to walk around our drawing-board takes us to our first innovation —television and film-aided design.

Bridging the Gulliver Gap

It was J. M. Anderson (Mackintosh School of Architecture) and H. E. Odling (Glasgow School of Art) who, in conjunction with the University of Glasgow television service, did much pioneer work in developing this approach to design. Their research project was based on the basic limitations of the commercial modelscope which, when used by the naked eye to view models, cannot isolate and focus upon particular aspects of a design and induces the Gulliver Gap —the term originally coined by Anderson. This refers to the toytown syndrome —the awareness of our own physical size in relation to that of a scale model, experienced even when peering down the thin tube of the modelscope. The need to both eradicate this unhappy intrusion in design and develop a method of exploring models so that their fuller implications might be made more realistic and accessible to others led to some exciting research.

Initial experiments centred on the design of the camera-model rig and methods of penetrating model spaces. Within the field at large there are two basic types of approach which relate to the investigation of interior and exterior space. In the interior model, the camera and scope are mounted under a table with the modelscope projecting in periscope fashion through a hole in the base of the model. In order to facilitate a moving image models are constructed without floorplanes so that they can be moved about the lens or, conversely, the modelscope head traverses the room on a trammel. In studies of exterior

1 Mackintosh School overhead rig for simulating movement through scale models of exterior urban space.

92

a

b

2 (a) Photograph of the actual
Mackintosh Room in the Glasgow
School of Art.
(b) Scale model of Mackintosh
Room viewed on a television
monitor. Note the floor channel
which accepts and routes the
periscope optics.

architectural space the camera and modelscope are mounted overhead on a movable gantry or counterweighted boom so that the sensation of walking or driving can be simulated (fig. 1).

After some technical improvements to the optical and electronic systems, a series of tests were conducted to determine the integrity of the televised image in conveying a sense of space. In order to check responses, different groups of subject/observers were asked to estimate a series of dimensions such as heights, widths and depths from a televised image of a real room, and a televised image of a scale model of the same room (fig. 2). It was significant that the subjects generally displayed a high rate of success in determining spatial dimensions from televised pictures of model spaces and, more particularly, that those who had no knowledge of the real space or of the nature of the experiment universally accepted the model simulation as a real space! In this way, Anderson and his team demonstrated that it was potentially possible to show observers a convincing and dynamic picture of an architectural space before construction, thus bridging the Gulliver Gap.

Further tests compared the relative quality of video tape recording with ciné film simulation and, in turn, their effectiveness with traditional drawings and models. This raised several important points. Firstly, the low definition of television pictures (especially black and white) tended to mask the lack of detail in rough models which the veracity of ciné film made apparent—a feature of television sets which in reality appear crude when compared with their softened appearance on the monitor. This pointed to V.T.R. as an ideal tool at the evaluative stage of design, with the added facility of immediate playback (as opposed to the delay imposed by ciné film processing). Secondly, that the addition of colour in both processes acted as an extremely important depth cue in simulated space. Thirdly, that although television and ciné pictures can convey dynamic illusions of space, they would not totally replace traditional representational methods but act rather as a powerful supplement to the inadequacies of drawings.

Although the television screen is a universally acceptable 'viewing' technique with a framework of conventions allowing the isolation, magnification and reduction of images, it cannot replace a visual perception gained by our physical locomotion through actual space. For the perceptual limitations of TV are those of any two-dimensional image which in being flat relies upon the secondary or monocular cues to depth with the addition of real-time motion and movement parallax. Also, in a model, the lack of aerial perspective may work against the acceptance of simulation. Furthermore, modelscope optics afford only a small field of vision and, in referring to the work of R. Sommer, Anderson points out that much of our experience of architecture is taken from areas beyond our focus of awareness. At any moment, we carry with us a spherical awareness of physical space—half of which is stored as memory in the brain of what exists behind us, while the other half is visible.

Nevertheless, Anderson's research has demonstrated that his system can enhance the value of physical modelling at all stages of design. Meanwhile, TV and film-aided design is undergoing technological improvements as a result of advances in electronics and optics which, apart from refining its visual, tracking and scanning ability, will reduce its hitherto cumbersome bulk to release the system as a portable design tool. Techniques of application are also developing. In Holland, for example, the Bouwcentrum in Rotterdam have evolved the Urbanoscope—a

3 Urbanoscope simulator, the Bouwcentrum, Rotterdam. Courtesy Rietveld B.V.

a

b

4 (a) Overhead rig, Berkeley
Environmental Simulation
Laboratory.
(b) Berkeley videotape image from
Improving the Street (phase IV),
Klock, O'Neill, Schmidt, Shaffer,
1977.

highly sophisticated commercial apparatus for viewing townscape-scale models
(fig. 3). In San Francisco, the Berkeley Environmental Simulation Laboratory have
successfully applied TV-aided methods to urban and highway design under the
direction of Kenneth Craik (Fig. 4). Other work in the USA is centred in Yale and
Washington Universities, and beyond architectural applications TV simulation is
used by the US Defense Department in war games and the training of astronauts by
N.A.S.A.

However, D. L. Bonsteel and E. R. Sasanoff of the University of Washington,
Seattle, are researching its application to buildings and, specifically, interior space.
Their programme sets out to refine the tracking patterns of the camera in simulated
space as a result of behaviour and movement patterns studied in real space.
Bonsteel and Sasanoff concentrated their study on the main gallery of the Museum
of History and Industry in Washington. Investigations began with an observational
study of the movement patterns of gallery visitors, individual movements being
plotted by drawing a line on a plan which was accompanied by comments
describing duration of time spent both within the space and with each of its
exhibits. After leaving the gallery each visitor/subject was interviewed to ascertain
his recollections regarding personal movement patterns and significant exhibits or
environmental features that he or she remembered.

Next, a large scale model of the space at one and a half inches to one foot was
constructed (fig. 5). As part of the construction, three-dimensional objects within
the gallery were replicated in scale together with a montage of photographs of
exhibits which had been taken in the real space and scaled down and strategically
located in the model —this possibility of using photographs for three-dimensional
representation had been suggested by commercial television where the camera, by
zooming into still photographs, is able to suggest the depth and reality of a scene.
Inside the model a hand controlled camera dolly was placed which could be used
to wander and see in response to the wishes of a viewer. The camera lens worked in

5 Scale model of the gallery in the
Museum of History and Industry,
Washington, Seattle.

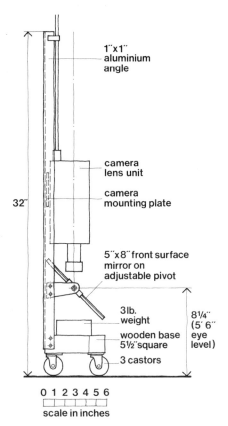

1"x1"
aluminium
angle

camera
lens unit

camera
mounting plate

32"

5"x8" front surface
mirror on
adjustable pivot

3 lb.
weight

wooden base
5½"square

3 castors

8¼"
(5' 6"
eye
level)

0 1 2 3 4 5 6
scale in inches

6 Camera dolly used in David Bonsteel's simulation experiment. (After a drawing by Larry Kaltman.)

7 Comparative movement patterns of actual and simulated 'visits' to the Washington Museum. The amount of backtracking required in simulation is compensation for the artificially narrow angle of vision.

conjunction with a pivoting mirror which could compensate for changes in eye heights and field of view (fig. 6).

For the second part of the experiment a further group of subjects who knew nothing of the research programme or, indeed, of what they were about to experience, were seated in front of the monitor screen in a simulation booth adjacent to the model. Each subject was invited to indicate his requirements for movement around the monitored space in order to explore its characteristics and contents via the television screen. Their directions could be overheard by a camera operator who manipulated the camera dolly in response to each request. Each route was recorded and on the completion of each visit (as with those in the real gallery) subjects were questioned about their route and their memory of its environmental features. After the test, subjects were acquainted with the simulation apparatus and Bonsteel and Sasanoff were fascinated to discover that, even after being shown the model itself, the majority of subjects still accepted the image on the television screen as an image of reality!

The Washington study had set out to produce a more naturalistic observation by camera of a specific environment and marry its vocabulary to that of the real world. It had demonstrated that it was possible to reproduce spatial movement in a television image but the greater amount of backtracking in the simulation (due to the narrow angle of vision of the lens) pointed to a pressing need —to develop an optical field approximating our one hundred and eighty degrees of vision (fig. 7). Post-test interviews further showed that simulated environmental features need not be necessarily realistic but that they should be consistent in their visual presentation. Bonsteel and Sasanoff explain that the modelling of environment is,

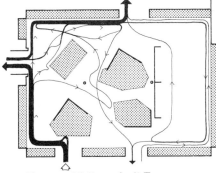

Museum Visitors: Left Turners

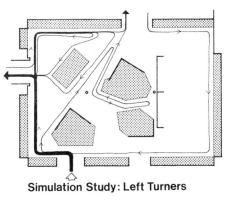

Simulation Study: Left Turners

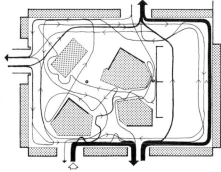

Museum Visitors: Right Turners

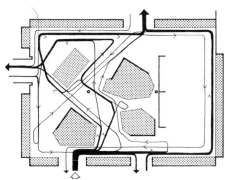

Simulation Study: Right Turners

8 Part of a Berkshire village rebuilt in miniature by a team of modelmaking enthusiasts—each with specialist skills. Courtesy The Pendon Museum of Miniature Landscape & Transport. Photo: Iradj Parvaneh.

'less a matter of exact duplication than a determination of limitations and capabilities of the television system itself'. They also suggest that the current model-making fashion with the continued popularity of model trains provides a resource of real things for use in models of a real world (fig. 8).

A key objective of this and, indeed, other simulation studies is the coupling of a continuity of viewing sequence with real-time movement, i.e., the ability to change or continue motion within a model space at the same time as viewing the monitored scene. The results of these studies begin to provide yet another laboratory check on behaviour in the real world.

However, as television and film simulation develops out of its infancy, its use offers a great number of advantages: it makes possible the viewing of proposed changes to the environment from the viewpoint of the designer, user and consumer of the proposed change; it also is a technique for considering design alternatives quickly and inexpensively and, when problems such as the small field of vision are overcome, it will become useful for more research into environmental issues of perception. But note the paradox that in its quest to harness the illusion of reality and movement to the design dialogue, TV and film simulation converts the three dimensions of models into a two-dimensional image on a screen. The next animated process of design in our review takes us back to drawings but this time those produced by a machine.

Cybernetic Space

The computer has, until recently, found it easier to process information than it has to present it. Consequently, it has proved itself of great value in solving functional problems in design but of little use in visual stimulation. Computers had acquired a bad name with architects because few could either understand or afford them: computers seemed unlikely to be of much use other than for the laborious problems of preparing and checking programmes; also it was feared that a machine might assume the role of designer or, at least, effect a standardized approach to design. Despite this short-sightedness, however, a computer technology harnessed to the environmental design process is developing at a fantastic pace, so much so that many of its newer techniques are in search of problems to solve.

With the recent evolution of relatively inexpensive visual display systems, the computer has been able to respond visually to architectural concepts of space. Such systems consist of a central processing unit (the brain), the peripheral display unit (the input and output terminal), and the interface which links the two. Whilst the size of a computers core-store (the memory) will affect the amount of detail which can be manipulated, it is the peripheral equipment which is of most use to the designer.

The two principal qualities of this equipment sought are: the type of information that it can accommodate, i.e., (in order of increasing complexity) letters, numbers, points, lines, curves, shading, colour and three-dimensions; and the degree of master-slave interaction, whether the designer can control continuously the computer's activites or whether, having set a task, he can only wait for the results.

The basic static display (output) is a machine which draws lines on a sheet of paper (the plotter). A drum plotter is the simplest to operate whilst a flatbed plotter is faster and more accurate. There are two kinds of dynamic computer display systems in common use: calligraphic displays which paint black and white pictures on a cathode ray tube—any part of the image being painted in any sequence—and raster displays, which produce tonal and coloured pictures painted in sequence like television images, i.e., from left to right and from top to bottom.

Three graphical input devices for instructing the machine can be used in conjunction with visual displays: a hairline cursor which can be moved across the screen, or a light pen (stylus) with an acoustic tablet (digitizer). Otherwise, the normal method of input is by keyboard, punched cards or magnetic tape. The programme is, essentially, a set of rules which are followed by the machine in order to interpret and apply the information it is given.

Realizing that the problem requiring most attention in computer graphics was the input technique, Donald P. Greenberg and his staff at the Laboratory of Computer Programmes at Cornell University decided to develop a system which would allow the designer to define any type of spatial information. Greenberg adopted the digitizing tablet as input because drawings can be made quickly and in freehand on it since the computer can, through a process called rubber-banding, automatically straighten them. The computer can also be instructed to ensure that lines are parallel and perpendicular, though continuously curved lines must first be fully drawn on the tablet. Designers can, however, overlay their sketches on the digitizing tablet and, after tracing-off the image, have it rapidly transformed into an accurate drawing (although some designers find this instant accuracy antagonistic to the design process). In creating perspectives, the computer can be programmed

98

9 Ambiguous boxes with five
potential variations in their
configuration all relying upon which
of the 'hidden lines' are removed
(after Josef Alber's *Structural
Constellations*, 1953–58).

to remove the lines and planes not normally seen by the viewer in three-dimensional drawings. These are mathematically erased using the hidden line routine which, therefore, creates more readable images (fig. 9).

The Laboratory of Computer Programmes has developed four input routines which relate directly to the generative and evaluative phase of design. The first involves the numerical description of primitive volumes such as cubes, cylinders or prisms or, indeed, any other geometric shape. Literally hundreds of these forms can be stored and recalled, multiplied, distorted, repositioned and built into structures —their composite image being viewed in perspective from any chosen vantage point. The second input is called serial sections—a method for the construction of free-forms based on tracings of required contours. A third method is a reversal of the process of creating perspectives; two photographs representing two different views on a building can be positioned on the digitizing tablet and, after touching the same detail in each picture with the stylus, the three-dimensional space between the two points is constructed. The potential of this operation is the determining of architectural component dimensions without the aid of working drawings. The fourth technique is called extrusion in which simple plans, via graphic commands, can be rotated to any desired isometric position. Walls and columns can then be extruded to required heights and the hidden lines removed by the machine.

Shading and colouring are not input techniques but display methods —although colours must be specified as input when the surfaces of an object are fed into the computer. Greenberg's cybernetic colour palette contains two hundred and fifty-six hues. Shadows, however, prove to be more complex to represent; a computer must first perceive the object under study from the point of view of the sun —the operator feeding in latitude, longitude and time of day. The computer then operates

99

a hidden surface routine to locate the fall of shadows before superimposing this data over the original description of the object in space. After typing in the observer's location (the origin of perspective projection co-ordinates being placed in the observer's eye) the machine repeats the hidden surface procedure to remove all unwanted lines and surfaces. Then, as long as co-ordinates such as ground-plane, elevation and horizon, etc, are defined, the computer is able to cast shadows.

The computerized graphic world created by such researchers as Professor Greenberg and his team is truly magical for it allows the designer to reshape rapidly concepts in space 'three-dimensionally', retrieve a variety of forms from a library of shapes filed in the disk memory and assemble them on a contoured site. Freeform contours can be combined with an object, then converted into a perspective, to allow the designer to zoom in and walk around the resultant space. Coloured forms can be summoned which, being illuminated by the sun, cast accurate shadows and, in turn, reflect light or receive shade from nearby objects. Using a programme called Stretch, linear networks, even if oddly shaped, can be visually inflated into three dimensions —at each stage of animation, a plan, elevation and perspective being furnished by the display and its final geometry being rendered in colour. It is, therefore, possible for the computer to describe hypothetical concepts of buildings in full colour and in three dimensions. These can be superimposed on to photographs of intended settings so that through a simulation of real-time movement the architect can explore visually the implications of his concepts of space.

The most realistic displays yet obtained have been via a colour television monitor and by filming sequences of computer-generated images. Such a process was utilized by Greenberg for visually exploring the potential siting of a new museum on the Cornell campus. His study employed a dynamic display system first introduced by General Electric's Visual Simulation Laboratory for N.A.S.A.'s simulation procedures designed to train astronauts for docking manoeuvres in space and landings on the moon.

A more exciting development would enable the designer physically to move around and within real-time perception of space. This stereoscopic illusion has become the dream of Ivan Sutherland who, whilst at the University of Utah, strove to place an observer in the midst of a dynamic representation of his spatial concepts. Sutherland's solution was to mount two miniature cathode ray tubes in a helmet, one positioned in front of each eye (fig. 10). The device is linked to a computer by three aerials which convey co-ordinates locating the position of the wearer's head and direction of his vision —the display processor instantaneously providing the correct image. Because the stereoscopic apparition remains stationary relative to the observer's movements around the space, the illusion is convincingly created that the objects are present in the room with him. The image appears as transparent and presented in glowing lines —the observer being able to move into appropriate viewing positions in order to examine particular features of the objects portrayed. This device, which is still in an early developmental stage, will even allow for a split-image which, through prisms, permits the user to view his projects overlayed upon the real world.

For architecture, the rapid improvement of computer technology and graphic displays has supported a variety of applications as interactive partner in the design

10 The 'helmet' worn in Ivan
Sutherland's experiments.
Courtesy Ivan Sutherland.

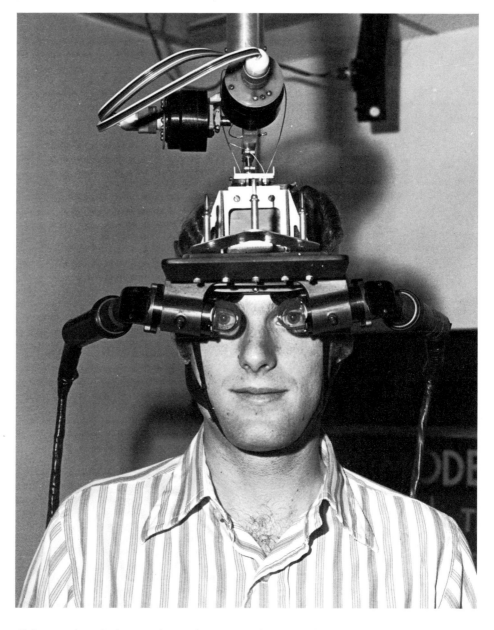

dialogue. In relation to the early stages of design, Nicholas Negroponte of the
Massachusetts Institute of Technology has been developing less formal
techniques using an electrostatic plotter. His concern with the perfection of
graphics resulting from the rubber-banding process has led him to design
programmes which enable the designer to doodle ideograms of plans and have
these less precise intentions interpreted by the computer. Meanwhile, the machine
begins to play a central design role in the profession at large. For example,
computer systems are in operation in the County Architect's Department of West
Sussex and in the Boston group of Perry, Dean and Stewart who use graphic
displays to determine relationships between various components of a building. The
Skidmore, Owings and Merrill office employs a computer which prints off graphic
descriptions of the overhead public railway system —the 'Loop' —in downtown

101

Chicago; these representations are utilized in preliminary design studies. Another Chicago landmark —the Sears Tower —had its interior design drawings generated by a machine-based drafting technique. This was employed to detail the furniture and phone layouts for its one hundred and ten floors by the firm of S.L.S. Environetics, Inc. This design group have found the machine to be particularly useful in repetitive operations —finding that the most complicated drawing (possibly taking one man a week to complete) can be computer generated in forty-five minutes (fig. 11). As early as 1962, S.L.S. began to investigate the possibilities of automated drafting. This led to the development of an in-house

11 (a) Portrait of the artist—Man-Mac. Courtesy SLS Environetics.

(b) *Opposite:* Furniture, telephone and electric plan drawn by Man-Mac for the Sears, Roebuck Tower, Chicago. Courtesy SLS Environetics.

102

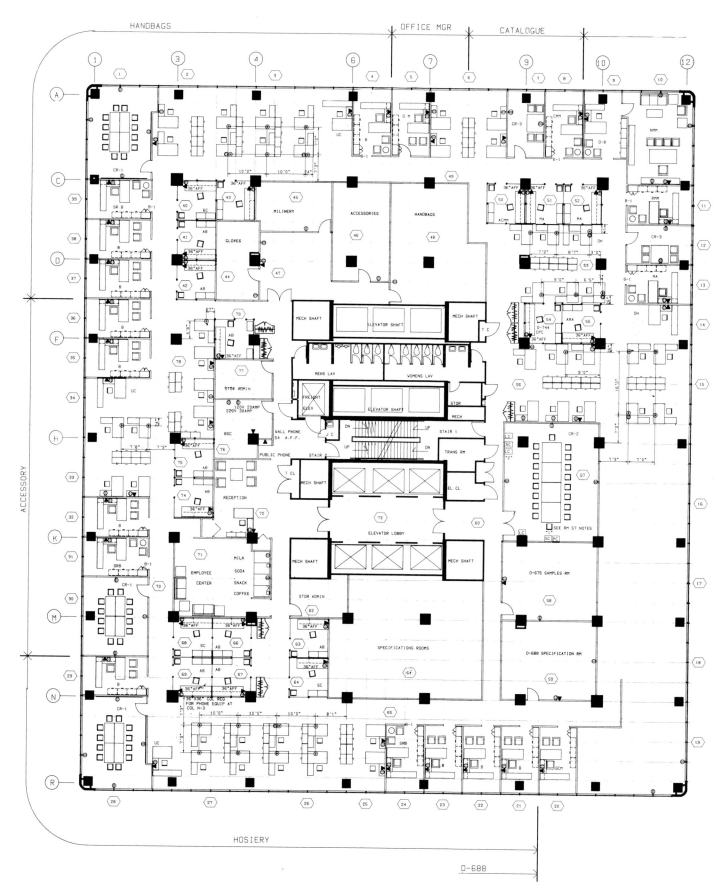

HANDBAGS   OFFICE MGR   CATALOGUE

ACCESSORY

MADISON STREET

HOSIERY

D-688

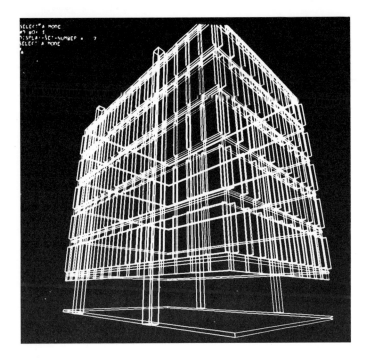

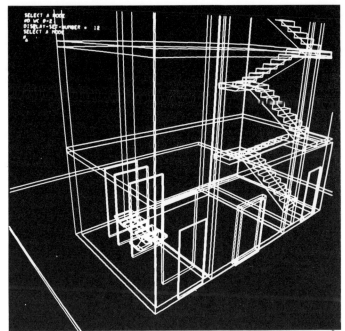

12 A street view of two façades of a small office building using a perspective display transformation.

13 A perspective display of the service core of the office building. Lavatories are on the left, stairs on the right.

These represent displays generated on a refresh vector display using BDS, a programme for modelling buildings developed by Eastman at Carnegie-Mellon University. Courtesy Charles M. Eastman.

system called Man-Mac through which they have designed more than three quarters of a billion square feet of office space. Lawrence Lerner, the President of S.L.S., defines the machine's role thus: 'Design is a discipline of function, logistics and economics moulded by aesthetics. The first three parts of this formula can be safely turned over to the machine, thereby freeing the designer for his most meaningful contribution, that of aesthetics.'

However, the use of the machine to create complete designs of buildings is at the heart of the work of a leading researcher, Professor Charles Eastman, Director of the Institute of Physical Planning. He and his team at the Carnegie-Mellon University in Pittsburgh, Pennsylvania are developing and implementing a system which is both capable of describing literally hundreds of thousands of architectural elements, and displaying and drawing parts of a design concept at different scales and levels of detail (fig. 12). The C-MU Buildings Description System (B.D.S.) is the result of this study; a system which is indicative of the future of machine-based design. A major effort of their programme has been devoted to the appropriate representation of architectural elements and, apart from physical components, the system is also designed to depict concepts of space as entities —even imaginary entities such as activity areas. A further property of B.D.S. is its ability to describe custom-designed, irregular and standard shapes with the intersection of lines, surface and volume being quickly computed and spatial conflicts easily identified (fig. 13).

Concurrent with Negroponte, Eastman and his researchers are moving towards sketch-recognition techniques which will allow the computer to conceptualize. However, Eastman's research holds other implications for the future for, in supporting a variable design approach, his system allows the user to initiate an idea with a structural module, the spaces to be enclosed, the external envelope, or other schema. By comparison to the side effects of the appearance of external information —such as in conventional architectural drawings, Eastman believes that the articulation of elements computed in three dimensions encourages a different way of thinking about design. The provision of this new, more realistic, mental perspective equates the importance of the invention of computer-aided design with Brunelleschi's invention of linear perspective. For it has not only freed the designer from the preconceptions associated with static drawings but opened new windows on his spatial thinking and brought him inside a concept that was, hitherto, inside his head.

So far, we have discussed moving pictures of design concepts either relayed from a source model or, via a programme, from a machine. The next section moves towards the creation of a physical, three-dimensional space through the construction of full-sized models:

Concepts to Full-Size

Experimental mock-ups as an evaluative aid to design are usually constructed from materials other than those intended for the ultimate form. For example, Michelangelo prefabricated full-size wooden replicas of parts of buildings such as cornices and had them hoisted into position so that he, and his clients, could assess their suitability before completing construction. Similarly, Sir Christopher Wren had a plaster copy of a piece of sculpture intended for St. Pauls Cathedral positioned on its unfinished edifice in order to examine its visual effect and as a check on its scale prior to the production of further sculpture. In 1972, when Oxford's City Council were considering the re-siting of the Carfax Conduit —a medieval water pump displaced from its original setting in the busy City centre — they had a painted canvas, wood and metal replica made and erected in a newly proposed site (fig. 14). After a period of deliberation, the mock-up was removed.

14 Carfax Conduit mock-up positioned in one of several potential Oxford City locations during tests in the unsuccessful attempt to reinstate the medieval water pump. Courtesy The Oxford Mail & Times.

105

14 (a) Edwin Lutyen's full-size wooden trial mock-up of the extensions for his design for Castle Drogo, Devon. Courtesy The National Trust.

That its new setting would be inappropriate was thus an informed decision. Canvas and timber was also employed by Mies van der Rohe in the fabrication of a full-sized mock-up of his Kröller House built on its site in The Hague, and Edwin Lutyens prefabricated in wood his extensions to Castle Drogo, to give his client a preview of its full-scale appearance. (Fig. 14 (a).)

The anticipatory simulation of full-sized architectural space can take on various forms, being used for different purposes and at many different stages in the design process. In 1959, when the Greater London Council were considering a planning application for the Shell Building, large balloons were positioned above the site-space as a method of identifying the upper limits of the proposed mass and its effect on the immediate environment. This simple method is commonly used as an aid in anticipating the effects of highrise buildings, for example, in the planning of the Magic Kingdom in Florida's Disney Land. It is also common practice for builders to erect a sample panel of brickwork on the building site for approval by the architect. Similarly, some of the shell roof units for Jørn Utzon's Sydney Opera House were mocked-up in wood to full-scale but for functional and structural purposes rather than visual reasons. A common practice in the United States is the on-site construction of one floor of a skyscraper before building commences, the prototype being utilized for experiments with lighting, services, detailing, colour schemes and furniture layout. As each of the floor spaces of a skyscraper are virtually identical, this process, economically viable for prestigious buildings, was used in the internal planning of the Seagram Building and Chase Manhattan Bank and the Union Carbide building in New York (fig. 15).

Full-sized working prototypes are more commonly used in industrial design in order to test mechanical performance and physical assembly especially where mass-production is involved. For example, in car design full-scale wax replicas are prepared for new models which are connected by sensors to a computer which,

15 Mock-up of one level of Skidmore, Owings & Merrill's design for the Union Carbide Building, New York, N.Y. The prefabrication was elevated so as to assess its perception from below. Courtesy Skidmore, Owings & Merrill.

106

after accurately recording the topography of its shape, feeds the data to the machine which fashions dies. Mock-ups are also widely used in the developmental design of ships, aeroplanes and spacecraft; the latter process providing a fascinating junkyard of cast-off hardware housed in the N.A.S.A. Museums at Washington, D.C. and Cape Kennedy (fig. 16). However, where mass-production of housing is concerned, full-size mock-ups of designs for individual units planned for extensive proliferation, might enable better public participation in their creation. One has only to observe the popularity of the site showhouse or the complete houses erected and dismantled for Ideal Home exhibitions to realize their value in communicating with laymen who find extreme difficulty in reading architect's drawings.

Depending upon the nature of the mock-up, all visual cues can be represented in space, obviously providing a high quality of visual information. It is also capable of introducing another missing ingredient from architect's drawings —people —the opportunity for the designer to articulate space against the reactions of intended users. However, the full-size simulation of architectural space is difficult to achieve at the conceptual design stage for it involves large-scale elements and requires considerable expense, time and space in production. Mock-ups, therefore, are only considered as probes into extremely delicate situations and enlisted exclusively by the more sensitive designer who cares deeply about the total implications of his intentions. Such designers include Skidmore, Owings and Merrill in the USA and

16 (a) Interior design mock-up of Skylab, Lyndon B. Johnson Space Centre, Florida. Photo: N.A.S.A.
(b) Mock-up of the Saturn 1 Orbital Workshop, Kennedy Space Centre, Houston. Photo: N.A.S.A.

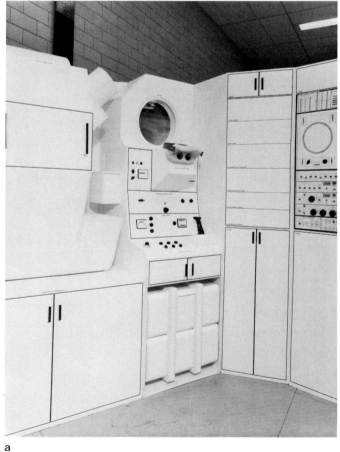

a   b

Foster Associates in the UK. The former prefabricate mock-ups constructed in the intended building materials as a means of checking a diversity of design aspects such as structure, internal function, fire-proofing and aesthetics (fig. 17). The latter rented a South London warehouse for the full-size erection of prototypes for the Willis, Faber and Dumas building, including sample columns, partitioning, lighting, ceiling and suspended floor systems (fig. 18). As a prelude to the construction of the Sainsbury Centre, University of East Anglia, Foster Associates initiated full-sized room fabrications, full-sized display system prototypes and full-sized cladding panels—first in silver painted timber, then in G.R.P. (Glass Reinforced Plastic) prior to the making of the machine tool for the aluminium panel production run.

The design student, however, rarely has the chance to experience his spatial ideas full-size (this being delayed until the reality of his first building) but full-size simulation might be provided by kit-forms, adjustable planes as in theatre or television design which is, after all, the sophisticated business of creating temporary, quick-change environments. A visit to any film studio lot will show the seed of this idea —heaps of components such as walls, doors, windows, and stairs; such a reusable vocabulary of elements for the rapid assembly of 'architectural sets' has been the dream of many designers. At the Mackintosh School of Architecture in Glasgow, J. M. Anderson instigated the design of a full-size, knock-down 'space simulator' to allow his students to test their own design concepts in some reality. Predictably, however, estimates of both space and money required for a system containing a reasonable range of choice were too high to allow them to continue.

Even at a basic level, however, spatial volume can be visualized using string simply to delineate the limits of a conceptual mass — and afford some comparison between scale differences in models and full-size. Depending upon their size such constructions could be quickly erected either indoors or outdoors using

17 Preconstructed full-size metal section of Skidmore, Owings & Merrill's design for the United States Steel Building destined for New York's Broadway. The photograph was taken prior to a fire test.

108

convenient walls, trees, or other horizontal supports, vertical or diagonal lines could then be weighted or pegged to the ground.

At a highly sophisticated level, one might predict the development of an automated space simulator in which one might command the dynamic articulation of solid and void —effecting changes in space, surface and colour at the press of a button! This might be housed in Simulation Centres accessible to both students and professionals —then mock-ups supplying the full range of sensory stimuli could be truly used at the outset of design. A close relative of this idea —at least, in degree of sophistication —is found in existing, highly sophisticated environments resulting from the mating of mock-ups with the computer. In 1970, Ivan Sutherland described his experiences with dynamic computer displays as a 'window on Alice's Wonderland' for, through them, he had 'landed' an aeroplane on the moving deck of a flight carrier and 'flown' in a rocket at nearly the speed of light. In the linking of computer displays to the full-sized mock-up we enter a method of simulation used in the training of boat, aeroplane and spacecraft pilots.

Simulators of this kind have become a way of life for a variety of reasons. They offer safety in training, operating flexibility and cost savings that a real-life training programme cannot challenge. One of the obvious attributes of the trainer simulator is its ability to create emergencies that would be hazardous at sea or in the air and fatal in outer space. For example, in flight simulators the weather conditions are controllable so that pilots can be gradually introduced to progressively deteriorating conditions. Modern flight simulators satisfy demands for total realism over the complete flight envelope with a flight deck that exactly replicates the real thing. The faithful mock-up of a flight deck comprises motion systems to obtain simulated sensations of large-aircraft movements, visual flight displays and computer systems. The other human sense fooled by flight simulation is hearing — engine noises and aerodynamic sounds being reproduced over the complete

18 Interior systems for the Willis, Faber & Dumas Building, Ipswich, erected to full-size by Foster Associates in a London warehouse. Photo: John Donat.

109

operational and speed range. The visual-system computer obtains aircraft location and flightpath data from the main computer which is capable of calculating, thirty times per second (rapidly enough to simulate continuous movement) the viewing angle of up to six thousand landing lights. The flight-deck view, assembled on a cathode ray tube suspended above the windows, is transferred with realistic infinity focusing into the crew's field of vision via an optical system of curved mirror and beam-splitting glass. In addition to runway lights, two effects which enhance display authenticity are horizon glow and runway surface detail. Objects illuminated by landing lights can also be simulated, and low-visibility weather displayed simply by changing input data from the instructor's control panels.

The Boeing Space Simulation Centre in Washington, D.C. utilized a further example of this kind of sophisticated facility. Computer-linked mock-ups of lunar landing vehicles complete with camera image mixing device and screen projection provided a normal field of view of approximately one hundred and eighty degrees. This allows the trainee astronaut to see through his window the changes in the moon surface in televised colour, as he approaches and manoeuvres to land. For the lunar training, Boeing had learned from their Lunar Orbiter experience how sunlight reflects off the moon's surface. There is no scatter as we have on earth since there is no atmosphere; the moon's surface reflects light at exactly the same angle as it is beamed. Boeing deduced that this phenomenon could spell momentary confusion for descending astronauts—possibly causing them to white out at certain points of the descent. In order to overcome this potential problem, Boeing constructed an extensive simulator in which to train a small group of astronauts. Their equipment occupied several rooms and comprised a surface that reflected light as does the moon, an artificial sun, a projection room, computer, and a landing module mock-up which simulated the landing (fig. 19).

19 (a) Views of descent stages from 5 000 to 1 000 feet over the Hadley Apennine Apollo 15 landing areas seen on a television monitor using the lunar simulator, Kennedy Space Centre. Photo: N.A.S.A.
(b) Astronauts Neil Armstrong and Edwin Aldrin practice in the lunar module simulator in preparation for their descent to the Moon's surface. Photo: N.A.S.A.

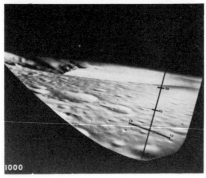

In its search for the simulation of a total space perception, the motion picture industry has developed from the silent screen via stereoscopic pictures and sound, in-depth focus (Vistavision), wide-angle screen (Cinemascope), full visual field (Cinerama), to the enveloping audio-visual attempts of multiphonic sound and circular screen (Sensaround). Other cinematic experiments into the widening of a celluloid sensory experience have touched on the possibilities of 'Smellies' and, as a step towards the tactile Feelies of Huxley's *Brave New World*, we have now entered the era of holography. This new medium, capable of creating three-dimensional photographs or complete pictures, however, holds implications far beyond the realm of entertainment. Its potential in the design process is possibly one of the most exciting innovations of our time for the ability to manifest images in space so that we can move around them is of the greatest interest to the designer.

Apparitions of Tomorrow

Holography was discovered theoretically by the Hungarian-born scientist, Dennis Gabor, in 1947 but was not developed into a workable process of reproduction until 1963. Then reality had to await the invention of the laser—the powerful source of pure or coherent light required to make a sizeable holographic recording and first utilized by Emmett Leith and Juris Upatnieks in the U.S.A. to successfully reproduce Gabor's original experiments. Theodore H. Maiman's invention of laser action in 1960 had transported the light ray from the fantasy world of science-fiction to a rapidly developing technology with a wide scope of application in industry, medicine and, paradoxically, in warfare. Holography is a fascinating facet of this technology.

In order to make a hologram, it is necessary to split a Laser beam into two parts. One beam (the reference beam) is directed via optical mirrors on to a glass plate (the hologram) which is covered with a special photosensitive emulsion. The second beam (the object beam) is simultaneously directed by mirrors to scan and record the dimensions and depths of the object under study. Where the reflected light waves emitting from the source object make contact with the waves of the reference beam, they overlap to set up an interference pattern which is then recorded on the glass plate (fig. 20). The plate is then processed as would be an ordinary photographic film. Its image is reconstructed through illumination by a laser beam directed at the plate at the same angle as the original reference beam. There are two kinds of holographic apparition: one producing a Virtual Image and one producing a Real Image. If the plate is illuminated by the reference beam alone, a three-dimensional representation of the source object is visible behind the plate—the viewer looking through the holographic plate, as if through a window. This image is called the Virtual Image. For the illusion to occur between the viewer and the plate—a much more exciting phenomenon—a more complex process of reproduction is necessary involving the recording of a second hologram. First, the original hologram is illuminated from the back by a beam of diverging light; the resultant three-dimensional image—known as a Near or Real Image—occurs and is viewed from the front of the plate. However, the configuration of this image is pseudoscopic or back to front as is a mirror reflection and, as the hologram is a three-dimensional recording, it also embodies a reversed perspective. In order to reconstitute its original configuration, the image is projected into space and rephotographed holographically. The projection of this

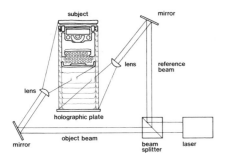

20 Plan of a holographic recording showing the laser beam split to illuminate the object (object beam) and the hologram (reference beam).

21 'Real Image' hologram. In this kind of apparition the tap appears in front of the plate. Photo: Theo Bergström.

plate creates an exact replica of the original subject in the space between the viewer and the plate (fig. 21).

Holography is the only representational medium which is capable of reconstructing all the visual properties of our perception of real space. Movement of the observer leads to variations in perspective; binocular eye movements register accommodation and convergence—disparity occurring naturally and without auxiliary viewing devices to focus or separate images. Objects hidden from one point of view may be seen from another as the viewer moves (fig. 22). An observer may, therefore, freely choose his point of focus and direction of movement. All secondary depth cues are also present in the apparition, thus including constancy scaling. Full colour images are still rather difficult to produce but, in principle, it will be possible to create an image identical both in size and colour to the original object. As with photographs, holograms possess no inherent scale. The images they present are divorced from their context and any scale can be implied by points of reference within the view.

The ability of a hologram to generate sequential imagery will be of great use to the designer. By recording an image and then recording another with the plate positioned at a different angle to the reference beam, a variety of impressions can be accepted, stored and generated by a single plate. There is no theoretical limit to the number of pictures acceptable to a 'Multiplex' hologram and this ability to generate sequential images, which is in effect a time-lapse facility, allows a build-up of information. Consequently, changing effects such as in light and shade, day and night cycles, or even colour sequences may be simulated. A design sequence from preliminary planning through spatial and structural organization to the architecture of the final form, may be overlayed on a single Multiplex plate. Superimposed visual information can also be achieved by two or more different holograms for, if two holographic plates are placed together, their individual pictures fuse to become one. This kind of projection could be employed to superimpose, say, an image of a building in model form and picture of its intended site; so that relationships of form and space might be evaluated in accurate simulation of the future reality. The more refined the model and lighting conditions, the more accurately would subtleties of surface and shadow be revealed.

The inevitable development of large holographic plates will achieve a more extensive viewing angle of the subject. If the plate is curved, for instance, it is possible to record a subject from all sides. By rotating the hologram or, by moving around it, an image of the entire subject can be seen. This ability to recreate our visualizations of architecture and position them in space so that we can walk around them, viewing them from all sides, is the promise of developments in holography. The future organization of a building will be materialized three hundred and sixty degrees in the round; planning will be carried out in three dimensions and spaces articulated in terms of their volume as perceived.

As current holographic methods are restricted to recording existing forms, at present design sequences must be carried out in another medium. For this reason, holography is seen by sceptics as merely a scientific novelty or, at best, a portable means of storing visual data from models. In this light it can only be used towards the end of designing, i.e., as a convenient means of storing and recalling three-dimensional illustrations of a design beyond completion in the design process. The making of holograms is an expensive activity but, like computer technology, it is

112

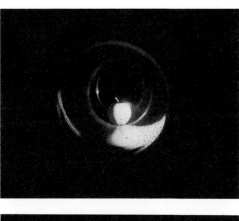

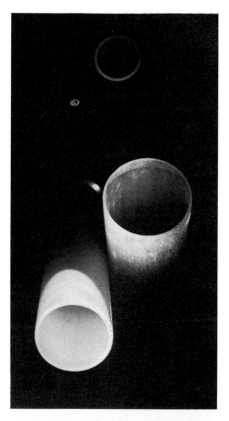

22 Series of views of an apple in a cylinder demonstrating the horizontal and vertical parallax of a hologram. Photo: Theo Bergström.

23 Pulse laser hologram projecting of 'Virtual Image', ie, a three-dimensional picture behind the plate, of two moving figures. Photo: Theo Bergström. (Holograms made at the Department of Physics, Loughborough University of Technology, Leicestershire, under the auspices of Holoco Ltd., Shepperton Studios, by a team directed by Nick Phillips.)

developing at a fantastic rate, beyond the Laserium light shows, Western shoot-outs of penny arcades, and the projected apparitions of Disney Land. Other, and possibly cheaper, techniques are now being developed which do not employ lasers in plate reproduction. Dr. R. V. Pole of I.B.M. has evolved the first techniques using ordinary white light. A multi-image picture called a Holocoder is reconstructed using a fly's eye lens composed of hundreds of different optical facets each producing a slightly different view of the field of study. However, the coherent light of the laser is necessary at some stage of the holographic reproduction process and when problems of restricted plate size, coherence of light source, and stability of image have been completely overcome —and researchers are confident that they will be —its ultimate mating with the computer will lead to the projection of abstract three-dimensional images. It is this development that will place holography in the hands of architects at the conceptual stage of design.

When this happens, the designer's awareness of his concepts of space at all stages of design will be almost complete. This near-future reality will not only aid decision-making within a profound awareness of space, but will deeply influence our perception of the environment and, indeed, our post-Renaissance concepts of reality!

At the very frontier of holographic development is Dr. N. Phillips of Loughborough University —a physicist who is responsible for many of the innovations discussed thus far. Apart from making important breakthroughs in the stability problem, he has succeeded in projecting a large Virtual Image more than twenty-five feet behind the plate, and even holographed a full-size human figure in motion (fig. 23). The rapidity of Phillip's developments reminds us that to discuss technologies in flux is to build upon a quicksand. It is vital, therefore, that designers keep in constant contact with the pace of events.

It is well-known that Joseph Paxton initially visualized his ideas for the Crystal Palace on a blotting pad; that Oscar Neimeyer drafted forms for Brazilia on the back of a cigarette packet, and that Charles Moore doodled a design idea on a table napkin. However, in the near future architects, as well as utilizing scraps of paper and the drawing-board, might also be externalizing their concepts of space on the digitizing tablet and, indeed, in the light of lasers.

Note
[1] Gibson, J. J. *The Perception of the Visual World* Allen and Unwin, London, 1950.

Bibliography

1. Design

Anderson, D.M. *Elements of Design* Holt, Rinehart and Winston, New York, 1961

Banham, R. *Theory of Design in the First Machine Age* Architectural Press, London, 1970

Beckwith, M. and Chelz, T. (Ed's) *Design Graphics 2* Kansas State University, Manhattan, 1978

Broadbent, G. *Design in Architecture* John Wiley and Sons, London, 1973 (New York, 1978)

de Sausmarez, M. *Basic Design: The Dynamics of Visual Form* Studio Vista, London, 1964 (Van Nostrand Reinhold, New York, 1964)

Itten, J. *Design and Form* Thames and Hudson, London, 1963 (Van Nostrand Reinhold, New York, 1975)

Kranz, S. and Fisher, R. *Understanding Visual Forms* Van Nostrand Reinhold Company, New York, 1977

Le Corbusier *For Students Only: If I Had to Teach Students* Faber, London, 1954

Licklider, H. *Architectural Scale* Architectural Press, London, 1965 (Brazillier, New York, 1966)

Lynes, J. A. *Brunelleschi's Perspectives: A Re-assessment*, Plymouth Polytechnic, 1978

Moholy-Nagy, L. *Vision in Motion* Theobald, Chicago, 1947

Papanek, V. *Design for the Real World* Thames and Hudson, London, 1972 (Bantam, New York, 1976)

Porter, T. and Mikellides, B. *Colour for Architecture* Studio Vista, London, 1976 (Van Nostrand Reinhold, New York, 1976)

Rasmussen, S. E. *Experiencing Architecture* M.I.T. Press, Massachusetts, 1959

Saarinen, E. *Eero Saarinen on his Work* Yale University Press, New Haven, 1968

Smith, P. F. *The Syntax of Cities* Hutchinson, London, 1977

Sweeney, J. J. and Sert, J. L. *Antoni Gaudi* Architectural Press, London, 1960

Zevi, B. *Architecture as Space* Horizon Press, New York, 1957

2. History

Coulton J. J. *Greek Architects at Work* Paul Elek, London, 1977

Coulton, J. J. 'Towards Understanding Greek Temple Design: General Considerations' *Annual of the British School at Athens No: 70* The British School at Athens, London, 1975

Gropius, W. *The New Architecture and the Bauhaus* Museum of Modern Art, New York, 1937

Hargreaves, P. H. (Ed.) *A Sketchbook in Art History* Leonard Hill, London, 1968

Harvey, J. *The Medieval Architect* Wayland Publishers, London, 1972

Kuppers, H. *Color Origin System Uses* Van Nostrand Reinhold Company, New York, 1972

Levy, G. R. 'The Greek Discovery of Perspective: Its Influence on Renaissance and Modern Art' *Journal of the Royal Institute of British Architects,* January, 1943

McCurdy, E. (Trans.) *Leonardo da Vinci's Notebooks* Duckworth and Co., London, 1907

115

Vasari, G. *Lives of the Artists* Penguin Books Ltd., Middlesex, 1965 (Viking Press, New York)

3. Perception

Bayes, K. *The Therapeutic Effect of Environment on Emotionally Disturbed and Mentally Subnormal Children* Unwin, London, 1967

Birren, F. *Color and Human Response* Van Nostrand Reinhold Company, New York, 1978

Clouton, N. 'On Visual Perception and the Representation of Space' *Architectural Science Review,* Sydney, December, 1970

Friedman, S. and Juhasz, J. B. *Environments: Notes and Selections on Objects, Spaces, and Behaviour* Brooks/Cole, California, 1973

Gibson, J. J. *The Perception of the Visual World* Allen and Unwin, London, 1950

Gregory, R. L. *Eye and Brain* Weidenfeld and Nicolson, London, 1971 (McGraw, New York, 1973)

Gregory, R. L. and Gombrich, E. *Illusion in Nature and Art* Duckworth, London, 1973 (Scribner, New York, 1974)

Hall, E. T. *The Hidden Dimension* Doubleday, New York, 1966

Hesselgren, S. *The Language of Architecture* Vols, 1 and 2, Applied Science Publishers Ltd., London, 1972

Johansson, G. 'Visual Motion Perception' *Scientific American,* June, 1975

Lewin, K. *A Dynamic Theory of Personality* McGraw-Hill, New York, 1935

Mumford, L. 'Agents of Mechanization and the Eotechnic Phase', *Environments: Notes and Selections on Objects, Spaces, and Behaviour* Brooks/Cole, California, 1974

Sommer, R. *Personal Space: The Behavioural Basis of Design* Englewood Cliffs, Prentice-Hall, New Jersey, 1969

4. Simulation

Albarn, K. and Miall-Smith, J. *Diagram: The Instrument of Thought* Thames and Hudson, London, 1977

Anderson, J. M. 'A Television Aid to Design Presentation' *Architectural Research and Teaching,* November, 1970

Anderson, J. M. 'Simulating Architecture' *The Architects' Journal,* December, 1972

Batterton, F. and Whiting, K. 'The Representation of Spatial Concepts in Architectural Design' Oxford Polytechnic, 1974

Benyon, M. and Benthall, J. 'Laser Holography as a New Medium for Visual Communication' *Icographic,* October, 1971

Bonsteel, D. L. and Sasanoff, R. 'An Investigation of a Televised Image in Simulation of Architectural Space' University of Washington, Seattle, 1977

Eastman, C. M. 'The Use of Computers Instead of Drawings in Building Design' *The American Institute of Architects Journal,* March, 1975

Greenberg, D. P. 'Computer Graphics in Architecture' *Scientific American,* May, 1974

Hurst, M. 'Japan's DC-10 Simulator' *Flight International,* April , 1977

Janke, R. *Architectural Models* Thames and Hudson, London, 1968 (Architectural, New York, 1978)

Negroponte, N. *The Architectural Machine: Towards a More Human Environment* M.I.T. Press, Massachusetts, 1970

Reed, D. 'A Walk Around the Drawing-Board: The Use of Environmental Simulators' *Synthesis No. 7* Oxford Polytechnic, 1975

Scott, F. 'Pictorial and Sensual Space' *Architectural Association Quarterly* Volume 8, No. 4, 1976

Sutherland, I. 'Computer Displays' *Scientific American* June, 1970

Wolff, J., Phillips, N., Furst, A. *Light Fantastic* Bergstrom + Boyle, London, 1977

5. Magazines

Architectural Design, Architectural Record, Design, Flight International, Icographic, Progressive Architecture, Scientific American, Studio International, The Architects' Journal.

116

Index